Stories of the
HUMBOLDT WAGON ROAD

ANDY MARK

Published by The History Press
Charleston, SC
www.historypress.com

Copyright © 2020 by Andy Mark
All rights reserved

Back cover, top: Chico and Humboldt Wagon Road Company stock certificate. *Courtesy of CSU, Chico, Meriam Library, Special Collections.*

First published 2020

Manufactured in the United States

ISBN 9781467145268

Library of Congress Control Number: 2019956040

Notice: The information in this book is true and complete to the best of our knowledge. It is offered without guarantee on the part of the author or The History Press. The author and The History Press disclaim all liability in connection with the use of this book.

All rights reserved. No part of this book may be reproduced or transmitted in any form whatsoever without prior written permission from the publisher except in the case of brief quotations embodied in critical articles and reviews.

Contents

Preface	5
Acknowledgements	9
Introduction: A Description of the Road	11

1. 1860s: The Road to the Mines

Overview	23
A Brutal Killing in the Desert	32
The "Mad" Rush for Black Rock Silver	37
Stage Robbery Near the Big Summit	51
Tollgate Violators, Human and Otherwise	53
They Knew How to Party at Camp Jones	54

2. 1870s: A Postal Route Established

Overview	57
Flirting in the Mountains	70
The Condition of the Road	71
Livestock Celebrate New Year Early	73
Bizarre Murder on the Road	74
A Curious Case, Indeed	77
The Soap Man Gets Robbed on the Big Summit	78
Accidents Along the Road and at the Mills	79
Harrowing Escape at the Sutton House	81
Tragedy on the V-Flume	81
Forest Destruction and Climate Change	83

Contents

3. 1880s: The Road Charter Expires

Overview	85
Harrowing Snow Stories	93
Mining for Gold Was No Holiday	99
The Racquette	100
Dashing Through the Snow	102
Dead Man's Hill	102
Billy Boness Still in the News	105
Scary Bear Stories	106
Sometimes It Was Better to Walk	107
Frank Mickey's Wild Ride	108
A Christmas Miracle	109
Shootout Near the Big Summit	110
Thrilling V-Flume Rides	113
The Hoisting Works	116
Put Your Head in the Hat	116
Tragedy Strikes the Cussick Family	118
The Government vs. Sierra Lumber Company	119

4. 1890s: Clashing Over Road Maintenance

Overview	121
Washington's Birthday in Forest Ranch	130
More Accidents on the Road	131
Another Scary Bear Story	133
Lizzie McGann	134
J.H. Shuffleton Dukes It Out in Print	136
Attempted Rape on the Big Summit	137
Mattie Warfield Has Close Call, Eventually Runs Out of Luck	139
Don't Mess with Earnest Bilby Collins	141
Runaway on the Tramway	142
Mountain Men on City Bikes	143

Epilogue	145
Appendix 1: Truth or Fiction	149
Appendix 2: Grand Views from the Humboldt Road	153
Notes	155
Bibliography	167
Index	171
About the Author	176

Preface

There is already quite a bit of information in print about the Humboldt Wagon Road, but I feel that not enough attention has been given to its early years. The primary intention of this book is to fill that gap in an entertaining way.

John Bidwell, more than any other person, was responsible for the birth, development and maintenance of the Humboldt Wagon Road for many years after it was first conceived. (It was officially named the "Chico and Humboldt Wagon Road" for the first twenty years, but it was mostly referred to in the news as simply the "Humboldt road.") Like many great men, Bidwell was a visionary, and he envisioned Chico as a major hub of transportation between Northern California and the rich mines of Nevada and Idaho. Unfortunately for him, the intercontinental railroad would soon destroy those aspirations. Nonetheless, the road was still a success, although not the grand one he had hoped for, and much of it is still in use today.

The Chico and Humboldt Wagon Road was originally developed as part of a dirt highway that stretched from Chico, California, to the mines of Nevada, Idaho and even Montana. Its official limits went from Chico to Susanville, California, a distance of about one hundred miles. This book, however, focuses mostly on the section between Chico and Prattville, about sixty-five miles. Just before Prattville, the Humboldt Road lost its uniqueness, as it met with two other major thoroughfares, the Humbug Road and a branch of the Tehama County Wagon Road, its main road merging with the Chico road about sixteen miles before Susanville.

Preface

I go outside of my set boundaries occasionally, especially in regard to the Black Rock Desert in northwestern Nevada, which played such an important role in the earliest years of the road. The silver rush that occurred there over a roughly two-year period was clearly a major part of Chico and Humboldt Wagon Road news stories at the time, but historians have covered little of it from a Chico perspective. This book will change that.

I also prefer to write about places that I'm personally familiar with, and the Black Rock country certainly fulfills that objective. I have an affinity toward the region, despite the somewhat inhospitable reception it has given me at times. One of the coldest nights I ever experienced outdoors was on the outskirts of a little town called Gerlach, located on the edge of the Black Rock playa, at about 3,900 feet elevation. I was working on the railroad as a brakeman. It was mid-winter, late at night and snow and ice was everywhere. I was told over the radio by the train dispatcher, who was located in Sacramento, California, to "dig out the switch" and move the points over so that a train we were meeting could be lined into the siding.

The temperature was below zero. The wind was howling like a pack of wolves. I felt like I could just as well have been on Mount Everest. The wind was numbing my face and hands. With a long, heavy steel bar with a chisel point on one end, I hacked away at the stubborn ice that had such an unyielding grip on the rail. I took out some fusees (red signal flares) and tried to melt off the cursed substance. The ice kept its formidable hold on the points. After about half an hour of going back and forth between chiseling and applying heat, and apparently making no headway, I dragged my chilled body back onto the locomotive and called the dispatcher, begging him to let us meet the train at the next siding, if at all possible. Well, I must have sounded pretty miserable because he saw it my way, which ended up delaying the oncoming "hot-shot" for a few minutes. While writing the story in chapter 1 about the military chasing the Indians in the dead of winter, I could personally understand how difficult the conditions must have been. I was lucky, however, because I had the chance to opt out.

Each numbered chapter in the book focuses on a decade, although the 1860s and 1890s are actually partial decades. That is because road construction didn't start until after the 1860s had commenced, and this book more or less ends where my previous one essentially began, in the mid-1890s. Yes, I'm writing a prequel. My earlier book was titled *The West Branch Mill of the Sierra Lumber Company: Early Logging in Northeastern California* and was published by The History Press in 2012. As the name implies, it emphasized the lumber industry, but the Humboldt Road was a big part of it.

Preface

This time, the focus is reversed. The road is the primary topic, but related logging still gets quite a bit of attention. This book is designed so that each chapter about a particular decade first gives an overview of background information about the road and then logging. This is followed by a selection of stories that are presented in more detail (again, with logging placed at the end), which include extended quotes colorfully written by editors or correspondents and which couldn't have been said better by anyone else. Each of these detailed stories has a subheading of its own that describes the topic matter.

Please keep in mind that most of the newspaper quotes come from weekly editions and are often reprints from earlier daily editions, which are unavailable today. Therefore, the implied date of the reported event may be misleading when the paper refers to it as "yesterday" or "this morning" or even when it mentions a certain day of the week.

This book offers a variety of subject matter, ranging from humorous stories to some that are tragic. Although this was written to entertain, it has an academic element, too, in hopes of inspiring researchers to go further with it. Most importantly, the book offers a glimpse into the past, mostly taken from the perspective of writers who were living at the time, which is my favorite way to learn history.

Acknowledgements

First and foremost, I would like to thank my wife, Jill, for her patience and support throughout this project. She traveled with me all over northeastern California and northwestern Nevada to visit historical sites and contributed much to my knowledge of the route with her keen observations.

An immense amount of gratitude goes to Special Collections at California State University, Chico, Meriam Library, which provided the majority of the images in this book. George Thompson and his staff, in particular Stefani Baldivia and Cheryl Watson, were very generous with their assistance. I would also like to thank Special Collections at University of California, Davis for permitting me to reproduce an image from the Eastman's Originals Collection.

I am grateful to those people and institutions that generously donated or loaned historical photos for public use to California State University, Chico, Special Collections. This list includes John Nopel, Frederick Stansbury Clough, Bruce Bidwell, Larry V. Richardson, W.H. Hutchinson, Randy Taylor, Larry Moulton, Glenn Dietz, the Lucas family, Alzora Snyder, Patricia Barry, Andy Osborne, Plumas County Museum, Bidwell Mansion State Historic Park, Butte Meadows/Jonesville Community Association and the Stansbury Home Preservation Association. Thanks to David Nopel for arranging to have more of the Nopel collection of historical photos donated to CSU, Chico, Special Collections after the passing of his father, John.

Acknowledgements

Thanks to Marti Leicester, who coauthored a book with David Nopel titled *The Humboldt Wagon Road* (Arcadia Publishing, 2012), for her advice and general assistance. I am grateful to Shirlon Dodge for providing a photo of her grandfather-in-law James Dodge.

Much appreciation goes to Shelby Rodriguez of the Museum of Fine Arts, Houston, who provided a digital copy of a painting by well-known western artist Frederic Remington and permission to reproduce it in this book. Thanks to Karalea Clough of the Nevada Historical Society, Reno, who allowed me to reproduce an image that also vividly illustrated the subject matter. I am grateful to the Library of Congress for having the Butte and Tehama County maps available online for public use.

Many thanks go to Marilyn Quadrio, director of the Chester–Lake Almanor Museum and author of a book titled *Big Meadows and Lake Almanor* (Arcadia Publishing, 2014), who shared her extensive knowledge of the Chester and Lake Almanor area with me and contributed some photos for this book. I would like to thank Holabird Western Americana Collections for providing an excellent digital copy of the Chico Gold and Silver Mining Company stock certificate.

California State Archives in Sacramento gave me some valuable information in regard to the Chico Gold and Silver Mining Company. National Archives provided documents that helped determine when Louis Ruffa first settled on his ranch.

Ron Cooke led me to some wonderful internet sources and contributed very useful maps. Larry Moulton offered some good insight into the lumber mills of this time period. Dale Wangberg, John Rudderow and Richard Burrill contributed a few news clippings that I used in this book and helped clear up some confusion in regard to the 1866 and 1867 stage robberies.

Ron Womack of the Association for Northern California Historical Research (ANCHR) and I kicked information back and forth in regard to the Ten-Mile House. Thanks to Josie Reifschneider-Smith, also of ANCHR, for her help as well.

Finally, I would like to thank Laurie Krill, acquisitions editor for The History Press, for guiding me through the process of getting this book published. Much appreciation also goes to Hayley Behal, The History Press copyeditor, for her help in making the book more presentable.

My apologies to anyone who provided assistance who I may have failed to acknowledge.

Introduction

A Description of the Road

The Chico and Humboldt Wagon Road began where Chico's Main Street joined a short section of road (eventually referred to as Oroville Avenue), which connected Broadway to Park Avenue. This was called the Junction, and there was an open area large enough to turn horses and wagons around for travel in a desired direction. The Junction was a hub for stages, pack trains and freight arriving from places as far away as San Francisco and Idaho. It was a busy terminal, and at one time or another, it had stables, blacksmiths, hotels, restaurants, saloons, drugstores, clothing stores, a Chinese laundry, a grocery store and other businesses to accommodate the land traveler.

People leaving the Junction eastbound for the hills found themselves immediately engulfed in dust during the dry season, as the road crossed over a valley floor beaten down and churned up by the hooves of bovines and equines and the wheels of the vehicles that were pulled behind them. During the wet season, this surface turned into slick mud, creating conditions that made it hard to keep vehicles from sliding around. Passing through this carpet of grassland interspersed with majestic valley oaks, the road roughly followed the course of Little Chico Creek, and a rider could begin the trip by viewing the lush riparian woodland—with sycamores, cottonwoods and willows—only a short distance away. If a person was lucky (or unlucky, depending on one's viewpoint), he or she might see a grizzly bear looking for a quick meal in the creek while squirrels scurried about the trees and vultures soared overhead.

INTRODUCTION

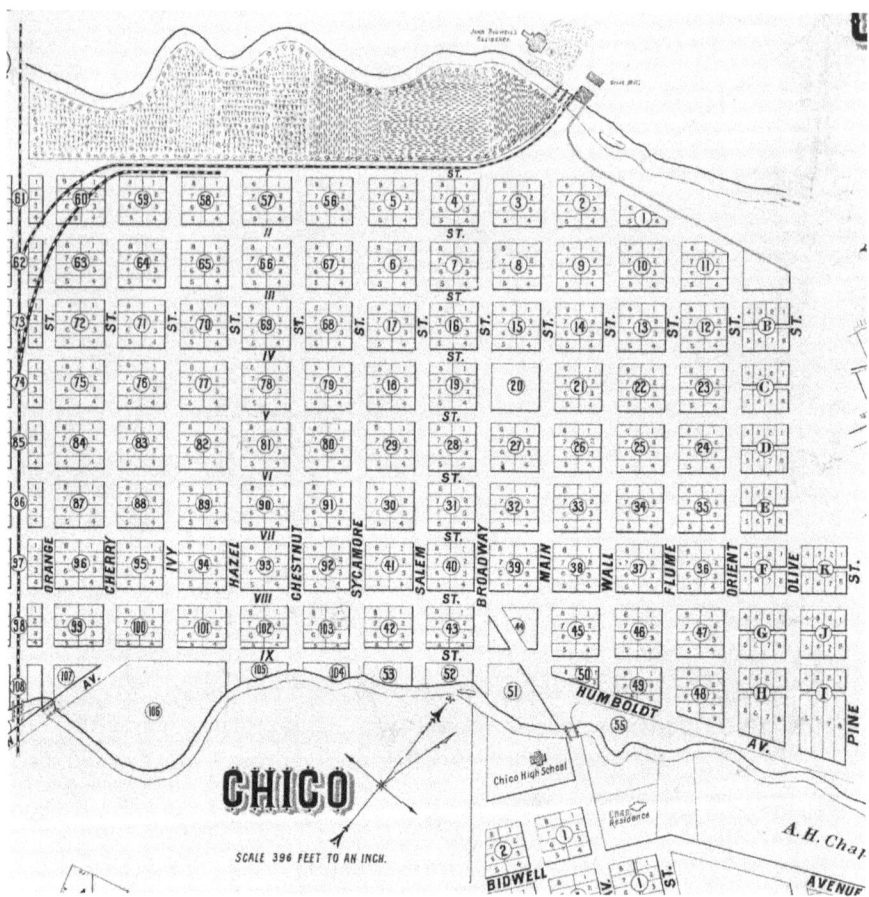

The Junction, seen in the lower right of the map. Bidwell's mansion is at the top. From *Official Map of the County of Butte, California, 1877*, compiled by James McGann. *Courtesy of Library of Congress.*

About three miles from the Junction, the road started to climb the foothills on a ridge separating Big Chico Creek and Little Chico Creek. As the slope ascended, the surrounding grassland was interrupted by a scattering of blue oak, with clumps of buckbrush and poison oak making a strong appearance. One might notice a few black-tailed deer feeding on the vegetation or a coyote trotting through the grass looking for a rodent meal.

Here, the surface of the land became hard and rocky—the solidified remains of the gradual breakdown of an ancient volcano called Mount Yana, which was located some forty miles away northwest, as the crow flies. The debris flows, called the Tuscan Formation, occurred one after another

Introduction

The Junction, with Main Street in the center, circa 1885. *Courtesy of CSU, Chico, Meriam Library, Special Collections.*

over an extended period of time between three and four million years ago. One can imagine how huge waves of mud and rock jumble streamed down the west slope of the mountains and slowly grinded to a halt. These were geologically violent times, and the remains were harsh as well. Riding over this bumpy stretch of road in a vehicle probably felt rough enough to rattle your teeth loose. To make matters worse, the iron-rimmed wheels of heavy freight wagons would gradually form deep ruts in the hard surface, which were very difficult to get out of when meeting an oncoming vehicle.

Speaking of annoying grooves in the ground, vehicles might also encounter a trench placed at a right angle to the road that was dug out to allow water runoff. Folklore has it that one of these was affectionately referred to by gentlemen stage riders as a "Thank you, m'am" because the sudden jolt from running over one may offer the opportunity to squeeze in a little closer to a female passenger sitting nearby. In fact, those four-wheeled wooden boxes with thick leather straps that stretched underneath the body of the coach to act as shock absorbers offered little in the way of comfort, so a passenger squeezed in next to you may have been your best cushion.

The first watering stop, at around nine hundred feet elevation, was about six miles from the Junction. It was called Hog Springs, supposedly because

Introduction

Riders packed into the Prattville stage. *Courtesy of CSU, Chico, Meriam Library, Special Collections.*

wild hogs used to quench their thirst there. One noticed that the gray pines, with their large cones and open, broom-like tops, began here. Throughout the early years of the road, a few refreshment and lodging stands tried to make a go of it at this spot along the road, but each ultimately failed, so most of the time, this was nothing more than a place to rest and wet your whistle. It was probably still too close to Chico for anything to be permanently established here.

From there, the road continued to ride atop the exposed Tuscan Formation, and as the elevation increased, the chaparral began to cover the rocky soils. Dense shrub, such as buckbrush and manzanita, joined the buckeye and live oak on the rising slope. This is where a rider might first catch a glimpse of a black bear, as hollowed-out logs, rock piles and caves became more available for resting or hiding. A mountain lion might be perched high on some rock outcropping, watching an unaware traveler's every move.

The next watering stop was about ten miles from the Junction. Because there were no wells or large springs nearby, an adequate amount of water was unavailable here until a system was developed that transported water in barrels from sources in nearby canyons. This was the closest location to Chico that eventually became a well-established way station, offering food, liquid refreshments, lodging (although meager) and a barn.

Introduction

A few miles farther, at about two thousand feet, the ponderosa pines began to overtake the gray variety before a mixed conifer forest quickly emerged with incense cedars, Douglas firs and sugar pines. Black oaks became more noticeable, and a few miles farther, tan oaks began to show up. As a result, the road softened a bit with pine and fir needles and oak leaves carpeting the ground. As the road passed through this harvestable timber belt, communities were established along the way with more meal and lodging accommodations available for a traveler.

The road continued to climb through the mixed conifer forest, and at about thirty miles from Chico, it began to ascend a steep portion before reaching the Little Summit, located about thirty-three miles from town at the 4,700-foot elevation. This was the first spot since leaving the valley where travelers would encounter an extended downhill. The view from this place was truly awe inspiring. Lassen Peak, only about thirty miles away, could be seen standing high above the rest of the wondrous mountain landscape. On a clear day, one would only have to turn a few degrees northwest to capture a view of the top of Mount Shasta, about 100 miles away, peeking over some intervening ridges.

After a descent of about one and a half miles, the road began to level out and roll slightly up and down through a stretch of woodland interspersed with lush green meadows. Much of this section followed the course of Butte Creek, and the next six miles would develop into a popular resort area with excellent hunting and fishing opportunities. Hotels, cabins and camping sites were readily available. It was a place where people from Chico could go to escape the brutal summertime heat of the valley.

Soon after, the road began another steep ascent to what was called the Big Summit (often referred to in the news as simply the "summit") at around 6,600 feet elevation and about forty-five miles from Chico. It was the highest point on the road, and winter snow could accumulate up to as much as 20 feet. The traveler was rewarded with another gorgeous panoramic view of the surrounding mountains. Again, one could clearly see the majestic Lassen Peak dominating the view to the north. From there, the road descended steeply around sharp curves and through a thick belt of red fir before eventually straightening out and dropping into one of the loveliest mountain valleys that a tired traveler could ever wish for.

At around 5,500 feet elevation, the bright green valley floor was nourished by a little waterway that passed through it called Butt Creek. Groves of quaking aspen trees lined the road and could be seen scattered throughout the lush meadowland. Pine trees bordered the roadway. The last established rest

INTRODUCTION

Introduction

Opposite: Fisherman at Butte Meadows, circa 1900. *Courtesy of CSU, Chico, Meriam Library, Special Collections.*

Above: Boating on the river in Big Meadows, circa 1889. *Courtesy of Chester–Lake Almanor Museum.*

stops before reaching Big Meadows and the town of Prattville were located in this valley. What a rejuvenating place it must have been. With towering mountain ridges above, one felt sheltered and could really think of the stifling valley heat as a distant memory. One can imagine what it may have felt like for a weary traveler to stop and relax at this place, where you can still sit underneath a grove of aspens and listen to the whisper of the cool mountain breeze as the rustling leaves move speckled sunlight across closed eyelids.

The Humboldt Road descended for about another fifteen miles or so, passing through pine forests and mountain meadows with little creeks full of tasty trout just waiting to leap into a frying pan. It eventually met with two other major roads (one coming from Oroville and a branch from another coming from Red Bluff) before reaching the town of Prattville. Located in what was then called the Big Meadows area, the original town of Prattville was about sixty-five miles from Chico and at around 4,500 feet elevation.

Introduction

(It was subsequently submerged when Lake Almanor was formed in 1914.) Prattville was another tourist magnet with a reputation for excellent fishing, hunting and many other mountain activities nearby. People from Chico often traveled to Prattville for vacation.

After making a steep climb out of Big Meadows, the road mostly passed through more pine forests and meadowland at a relatively constant elevation but with a few more steep hills along the way, until it finally reached the town of Susanville on the drier eastern slope of the Sierras, at around 4,200 feet elevation and about one hundred miles from Chico. Nearby was Honey Lake, a dry lakebed for part of the year. This country was where the pine trees came to an end and the sagebrush began to dominate.

Travelers headed to Idaho or Nevada from Susanville would generally follow Noble's Emigrant Trail for a way. At first, the terrain was dry and mostly grassland with few trees. About forty-five miles from Susanville, the road arrived at Rush Creek, where a reliable water source was available year-round. There was good camping here, too, with large cottonwood trees providing much-needed shade.

The second Prattville hotel was constructed in 1877, after the first one burned down. *Courtesy of Chester–Lake Almanor Museum.*

Introduction

Spliced together photos giving a panoramic view of Susanville, with Main Street on the left, circa 1885. *Courtesy of Special Collections, UC Davis Library.*

Eventually, the road wound its way through Smoke Creek Canyon. After leaving the small gorge, one was presented with an awe-inspiring view of an expansive wasteland directly ahead. This is now referred to as the Smoke Creek Desert, a roughly thirty-five-mile-long and, at some places, eight- to nine-mile-wide playa. For much of the year, the floor of the dark cream to white basin is dry and cracked. It is made of sediments deposited by the ancient Lake Lahontan during the last Ice Age and is devoid of life, thanks to thousands of years of evaporation that concentrated minerals and salts into an inhospitable environment for plants and animals. Following the northwestern edge of this salt flat for almost forty miles, the road traveler would take advantage of springs located along the way before finally arriving at what is now called the Black Rock Desert, an even larger playa left over from that same ancient lake.

The weather conditions in this land can be unforgiving. In the summer, you often have to contend with hot days and cold nights. When the sun is out, you may find yourself acting like the rest of the desert creatures, seeking shade, any shade. Fickle winds can persist for days, sucking the moisture from your body until you feel like an old, dried-up piece of toast. It's a place where dust devils dance across the desert floor like ghostly ballerinas and dust storms can envelop a wandering soul like a thick blanket of fog, making it difficult to breathe.

In the winter, it's just downright cold all of the time. Snow accumulations may not be deep, but the windchill factor clearly makes up for it.

The Black Rock Desert is probably best known for its highly publicized annual Burning Man festival that, since 1990, has taken place every summer around Labor Day. However, did you know that the sound barrier

Introduction

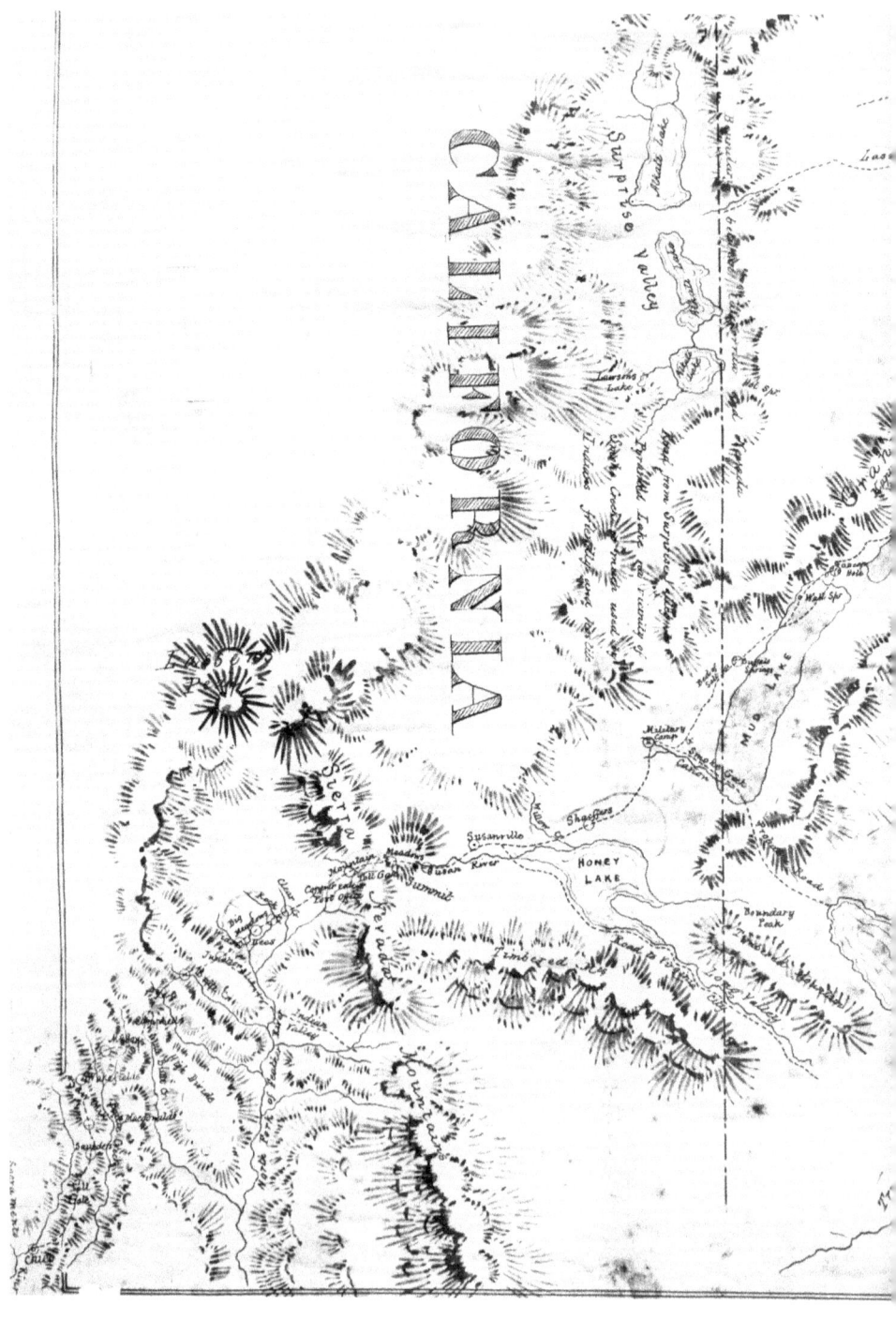

Introduction

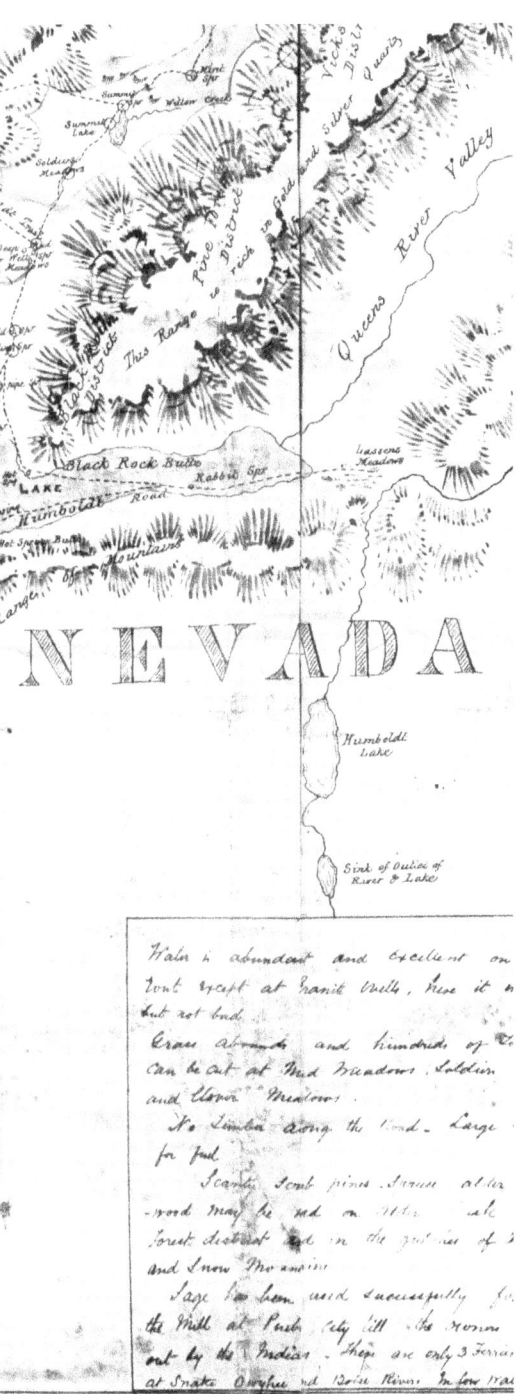

was first officially broken on land on this playa? A jet-propelled car named Thrust SSC scooted across the desert floor at about 763 miles per hour in October 1997. There was much anticipation and some anxiety prior to the event because, for one thing, no one knew for sure what would happen to the supersonic car when it reached the sound barrier. There was uncertainty about whether the shockwaves from breaking the barrier might flip the vehicle over and send it careening upside-down across the desert floor at more than 700 miles per hour. Thankfully, that did not happen. The British driver, Andy Green, survived. His reward for this brave feat was a prominent place in the record books. Now that was a historical event.

Travelers on the Chico and Humboldt Wagon Road who were headed for Idaho and the Humboldt mining district would go beyond this area. However, our description of the old highway ends here, simply because the stories in this book essentially go no farther.

Road from Chico to the Black Rock Desert. From 1865 map sketched by Captain John Mullen (spelled "Mullan" in the news). *Courtesy of CSU, Chico, Meriam Library, Special Collections.*

1

1860s

The Road to the Mines

OVERVIEW

History tells us that, from early adulthood, John Bidwell was an adventurous person who was willing to take some risks. At twenty-one years old, in the spring of 1841, he became a member of the first group of American settlers traveling overland to a region that was eventually named the state of California. (At that time, it was still Mexican territory.) The expedition was later known as the Bidwell-Bartleson Party because John Bidwell played a major role in organizing the journey and John Bartleson was elected captain.

The inexperienced California-bound travelers faced many hardships along the way on a trail that was not yet established. They had to cross an unforgiving, barren desert and were forced to negotiate steep, narrow and winding canyons to climb up and over high mountain passes. When they reached northeastern Nevada, they abandoned their wagons and had to pack their goods on oxen. Loss of livestock and shortage of food was commonplace. By the time the exhausted travelers arrived at their destination near San Francisco Bay on November 4, they had journeyed almost six months and covered about two thousand miles.

In late 1841, Bidwell landed a job with John Sutter, who was developing a settlement called New Helvetia near the confluence of the American and Sacramento Rivers. The fort that Sutter soon built there was to become the gateway for overland explorers arriving in California from

1843 to the end of the decade. Sutter immediately recognized Bidwell's strong character and many talents and soon made him his right-hand man, creating assignments for the young employee that ranged from bookkeeping to managing various enterprises that required Bidwell to travel all over Northern California. For the next eight years, Bidwell acquired some important experiences under the direction of Sutter, something that he would find useful in his own future enterprises.

In 1843, some horses were stolen from Bidwell not far from Sutter's Fort. To retrieve his lost livestock, Bidwell followed the guilty party up through Northern California. Along the way, he passed through a most beautiful and fertile region some ninety miles north of Sutter's, of which he quickly became enamored. This was the site of the future Rancho Chico in Butte County, the place that would eventually put Bidwell on the map.

In 1845, Bidwell purchased some land on the Farwell grant, which provided him a foothold in the area he had fallen in love with earlier. Bidwell built a small cabin on this land along Little Butte Creek and began to occupy the dwelling in 1847.

It was during the following year that possibly the most momentous event in California's recorded history occurred—the discovery of gold at Sutter's Mill in Coloma. Bidwell even had a hand in this. He was the one who drew up the contract between Sutter and James Marshall for the construction of the lumber mill. So, it seems appropriate that Bidwell would eventually strike it rich on the Middle Fork of the Feather River during the years 1848 and 1849. Not only was he successful at prospecting, but his business mind also went to work. He opened a store at the location, which made a healthy profit of its own. (Ironically, the subsequent widespread environmental destruction created by corporate-owned mines caused massive soil erosion to fill waterways all the way to the valley and prompted Bidwell to later become one of the mining industry's biggest critics.)

With his newfound wealth, John Bidwell purchased more land and, by 1851, was sole owner of Rancho Chico, a vast spread of ground 22,214 acres in size situated just north of the Farwell grant. Over the next decade, Bidwell developed a large agricultural operation on his rancho. During much of this time, he was still holding the land under a Mexican land grant, but he was eventually awarded a U.S. patent in 1860. That same year, he laid out and founded the town of Chico south of the agricultural area as a place for his employees to live and buy goods. He would eventually sell or give away almost all his properties on the Farwell grant while keeping most of Rancho Chico.

1860s: The Road to the Mines

John Bidwell struck it rich at a place that was eventually named after him, Bidwell Bar. *From Coy's 1925 book*, Pictorial History of California.

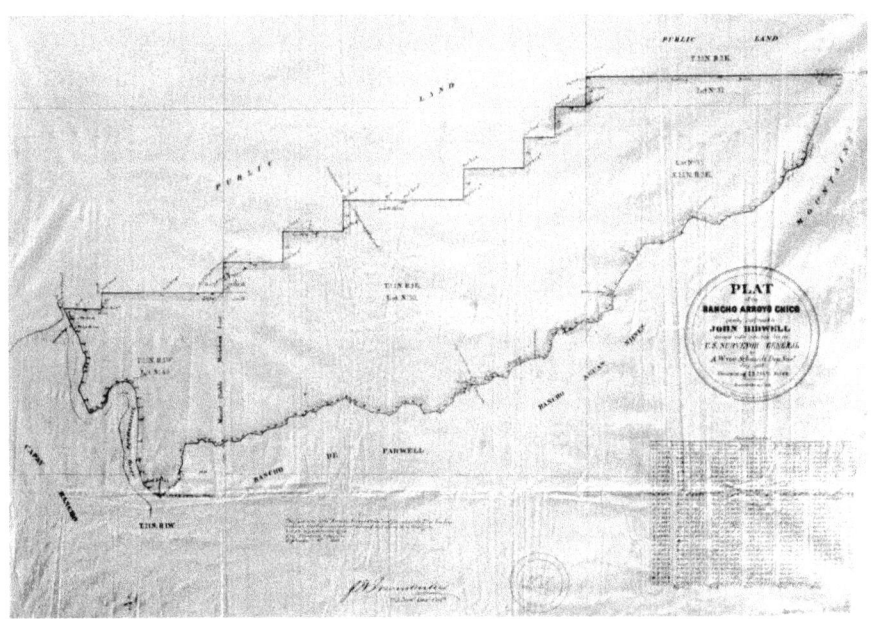

Plat of Rancho Arroyo Chico, surveyed in 1859. *Courtesy of CSU, Chico, Meriam Library, Special Collections.*

Portrait of John Bidwell, taken in 1860. *Courtesy of CSU, Chico, Meriam Library, Special Collections.*

Bidwell soon recognized the importance of creating conditions to secure Chico's future, and when news got out about rich silver strikes along the Humboldt Range, Nevada Territory in 1861, he thought it might be a good idea to get in on the action. Shortly afterward, Bidwell proposed a trans-Sierra wagon road, with Chico as the valley terminal, to connect Nevada's burgeoning mining industry with California. Not only would this operation put Chico in the enviable position of becoming a principal connection in a supply line between northwestern Nevada mines and San Francisco and beyond, but it would also give Bidwell a greater opportunity to ship products from his expanding field crop, orchard and livestock business.

In 1862, another mining boom was reported in southwestern Idaho, giving even more impetus to the establishment of a major transportation line from the valley to the Nevada and Idaho mining regions. Roadwork began that year. In September, it was reported that Bidwell managed to punch a sixty-five-mile road from Chico over the Sierras to deliver freight to the Humboldt mines,[1] suggesting the portion to Prattville was open.

In April 1863, John Bidwell and four others (J.C. Mandeville, R.M. Cochran, E.B. Pond and John Guill) received a twenty-year franchise from the state legislature to build and operate a toll road between Chico and Susanville in the Honey Lake Valley of northeastern California, where it would connect to a federal wagon road that went eastward to the Big Bend of Nevada's Humboldt River and beyond. Later that spring, it was advertised that pack trains, droves of cattle and wagons were crossing the road on a daily basis.[2] One paper reported that over six thousand head of cattle were on their way to the Humboldt mines.[3]

In 1864, the Chico and Humboldt Wagon Road Company was incorporated, and the name reflected the original intent of the enterprise. Bidwell was the wealthiest person in the Chico area and was the chief stockholder of the corporation. By the end of 1864, stagecoaches were also moving over the mountains from Chico to Susanville.

1860s: The Road to the Mines

It should be noted that in September 1863, during the Civil War, Governor Leland Stanford appointed John Bidwell to the position of brigadier general in the state militia. The new commander's primary responsibility was to suppress any threat of a Confederate uprising in California. Thereafter, Chico's founder was referred to as "General" Bidwell.

In the winter of 1864 and into 1865, three Idaho businessmen, J.B. Francis, E.D. Pierce and G.C. Robbins, formed the Idaho Stage Company and were looking for a connection into California from the southwestern corner of their state. Naturally, Bidwell thought it would be a great opportunity if the Idaho road connected with his own to make Chico the western terminal. Competing with Red Bluff and its more northern route to the Sacramento Valley was not easy because the way to Tehama County clearly had its advantages. But Bidwell may have swayed the decision by doing just about anything within reason to have his way. As it turned out, he gave the Idaho group substantial financial aid in the way of livestock, hay, harnesses and stagecoaches.

On April 3, 1865, the first saddle train traveled the road from Chico to Ruby City, Idaho,[4] taking twenty-seven days. After some problem areas were worked out (including changing sections of the route), the travel time was reduced considerably, with one party in June reportedly cutting it in half. Through traffic commenced sometime later that year, but there were troubles from the start, including periodic American Indian raids and lack of road maintenance. Well-known roadbuilder Captain John Mullan, who joined the operation in July, managed to get more military protection against natives, but they still caused trouble for travelers. Finally, the whole line was discontinued in the fall of that year. It was not prepared for winter travel anyway.

Early the next year, news of another mineral strike in the Black Rock Desert in northwestern Nevada fueled more enthusiasm for reopening the road. When the ambitious General Bidwell, by then a member of the U.S. House of Representatives, used some of his political clout to obtain a federal mail contract between Idaho and Susanville while switching the western terminus of the Susanville contract from Oroville to Chico, things began to look really rosy for his new road.

By April 1866, news began to emerge of freight and passenger travel out of Chico for destinations in Nevada, Idaho and Montana. It was reported that the way northward was being opened by none other than the well-known Indian fighter Hi Good and his train of five wagons and fifty pack animals.[5] One thing was for sure—Hi Good wasn't going to be intimidated by any hostile Nevada Indians. The tall, muscular man, who was considered by many at the time to be a regional hero, had already made quite a name for himself by killing many American Indians in California's Butte and Tehama Counties. Good was eventually killed by an orphaned Indian boy who he was raising at the time.[6] (Evidence suggests the boy likely had accomplices.)

After catching a good deal of heat from the press for failing to immediately come up with a magical solution to the Susanville-Idaho road problems of 1865, Captain John Mullan[7] was back in action the following spring. He was described by Chico's local press as "a small steam engine, and things move when he hitches to them."[8] On July 1, the new mail contract went into effect, and the first regular coach left Chico for Ruby City. The news later reported that the trip took three days and five hours.[9] It wasn't long before stages were leaving Chico for Idaho every other day.[10]

Earlier that spring, the Chico newspaper reported that the distance between Chico and Ruby City was 401 miles and published distances between the stations along the way.[11] One might wonder how they calculated mileage in those days. Well, it wasn't much different than today—with odometers attached to the wheels of a vehicle, such as a coach.[12]

In light of the competition with other local roads, it's interesting to note that if you believed everything the Chico newspaper had to say, its road couldn't be beat. Of course, newspapers from other towns would have the same glowing reports of their thoroughfares. Although Red Bluff's Tehama County Wagon Road and Oroville's Humbug Road were the nearest competitors for the westernmost section of the highway to Idaho,[13] they all shared a rivalry with the dominant Oregon Steam Navigation Company, which moved merchandise north from San Francisco, over the ocean, up the Columbia River, across the Blue Mountains and into the Idaho Basin. Chico's *Courant* newspaper never passed up a chance to report criticism of the steam company's path, commonly referred to as the "Webfoot" route, in which cargo had to be loaded and unloaded several times, risking damage to the goods.[14]

Despite continued Indian attacks, traffic was substantial on Bidwell's road for the rest of the year, until the first heavy snows of November. In March 1867, it was reported that the mail contract was cancelled.[15] When this was combined with the completion of the western portion of the Central Pacific Railroad track up to the big bend of the Humboldt River, allowing the distance by stage to be essentially cut in half, the demise of the Chico to Idaho stage route became obvious. The inevitable completion of the transcontinental railway in 1869 was the final nail in the coffin.

1860s: The Road to the Mines

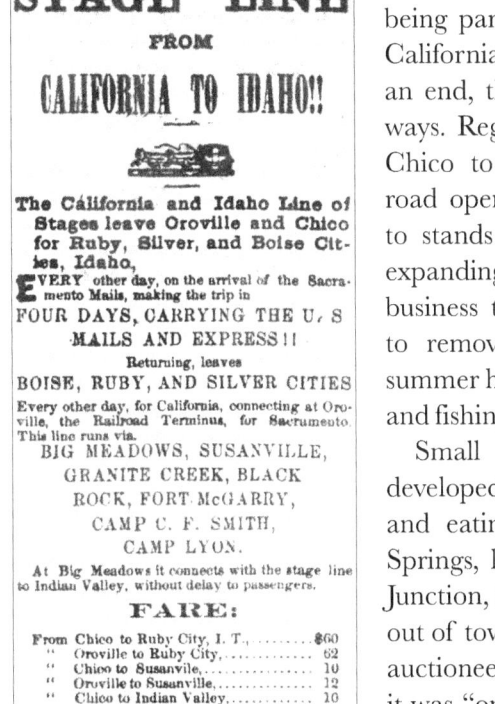

This *Chico Courant* ad, dated December 28, 1866, ran from the summer of 1866 to soon after the mail contract was discontinued early the following year.

While Bidwell's dream of Chico being part of a major supply route from California to Nevada and Idaho came to an end, the road was still useful in other ways. Regular stage traffic to points from Chico to Susanville continued, and the road opened the foothills and mountains to stands of virgin timber to supply an expanding logging industry. The resort business thrived as people used the road to remove themselves from the stifling summer heat of the valley and fine hunting and fishing opportunities became available.

Small settlements and hotels were developed along the way to furnish resting and eating stops for the travelers. Hog Springs, located about six miles from the Junction, in Chico, was the first water stop out of town. R.H. O'Ferrall, Butte County auctioneer, had it for sale in 1867, claiming it was "one of the best and most desirable stands on the road."[16]

Paul and Ellen Lucas settled on a small piece of land in Big Chico Creek Canyon, about fourteen miles from Chico (located in today's Big Chico Creek Ecological Reserve). The couple soon started raising children there, while creating a stock and butchering business.

Someone had to pay for repair and maintenance of the new wagon road. Who better than the people who actually used it? A tollgate, sometimes referred to as Cement Springs, was located some fourteen miles from Chico,[17] just up the road from the Lucas house.

Elias Findley's place, about sixteen miles away, had a garden that provided cold watermelon. Just two miles above Findley's was Saunders's place. McDonald's place was two miles beyond Saunders's. In 1867, it was reported that a fine two-story hotel was kept there by J.C. Wertsbaugher. The water was taken from a well sixty feet deep at a temperature of forty-

By the summer of 1867, new ads came out promoting local travel only, like this one from the *Chico Courant*, dated September 20, 1867.

six degrees. Captain Johnson had a mining claim nearby, as did some others. J.N. McCormick took over the place in 1868.[18]

Next was Wakefield's station (also known as Twenty-Four Mile House). When Henry Wakefield had the place for sale in 1866, he advertised it as a hotel station that had a house, a barn and outbuildings on the site with good water, a nice garden spot and a place to set up a mill, with plenty of timber on the acreage.[19] A year later, there were about half a dozen cabins here as well.

About thirty miles from Chico was a place on the ridge called the Hog's Back, so named because the terrain resembled the back of a swine, with Big Chico Creek running along the bottom of a canyon on one side and the West Branch of Butte Creek flowing below on the other. It was reported in 1867 that James K. Sprague kept a hotel there with stables and a blacksmith shop. He also had a water-powered shingle mill, which he managed to rebuild after the original burned down.[20]

Beyond Sprague's, the road soon became very steep as it ascended up to and over the Little Summit. Approximately thirty-six miles from Chico was the McGann ranch, situated in an area of woods interspersed with large, green meadowland. Butte Creek and its excellent fishing was nearby.

It was about six or seven miles from McGann's to the next place, at first called Campbell's. Later in the decade, the area was referred to as Camp Jones before the occupants finally settled on the name Jonesville. Here, hunting and exporting of skins was considered the primary occupation, but the place quickly became a summer retreat.[21]

About seven or eight miles past that, crossing over the Big Summit, was Dye's ranch, located at the beginning of a long stretch of mountain meadows that was interspersed with aspen and pine trees. In the winter of 1867, Dr. Sproul informed Susanville's newspaper, the *Sage Brush*, that it took

1860s: The Road to the Mines

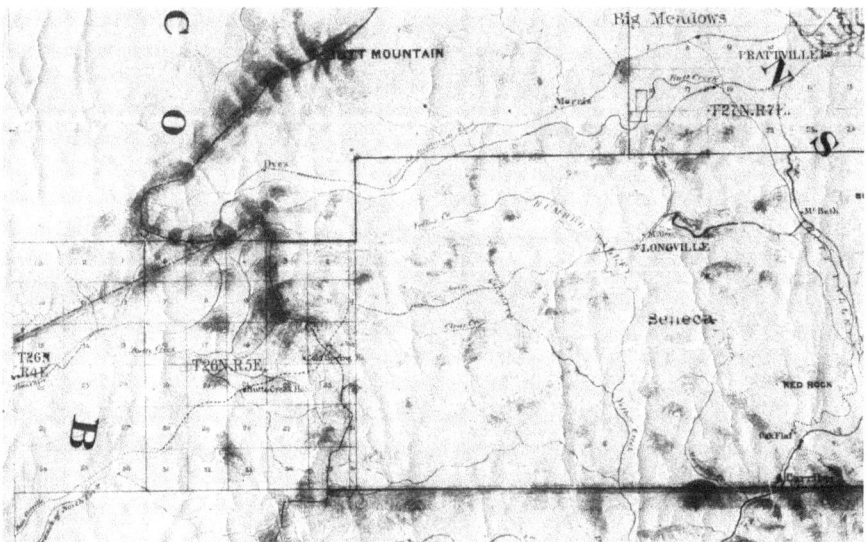

The Chico and Humboldt Wagon Road passed Dye's place on the way to Prattville. The road from Oroville can be seen south of the one from Chico. From *Official Map of Plumas County, 1874*, by Arthur Keddie. *Courtesy of CSU, Chico, Meriam Library, Special Collections.*

him sixteen hours travel time, while stopping overnight at Dye's, to go from Chico to Susanville on the stage.[22]

Dye's was a busy place, and in 1866, there was no shortage of excitement. In July, it was reported that a big grizzly was captured there by a trap baited with fresh meat. At the time of the news story, the bruin was still in the cage awaiting its fate, which did not look very promising.[23] Dye's place was also the scene of a rearrest. In October, a couple of prisoners broke out of the Susanville jail, and officers from Lassen County decided to take the stage for Chico and layover at Dye's to wait for the jailbirds, who would be passing by. Their hunch was right. It wasn't long before the fugitives were returned to Susanville to face trial on burglary charges.[24]

While the mail contract was still in effect, it was important to keep the entire line in operation at any expense. In 1867, it was reported that James Mack, the proprietor of the stage line, kept eight to twelve horses, with sleds, on the summit to keep the road open for mail and passengers.[25]

In the general vicinity of the McGann place, a side road left the main highway and, one and a half miles north, arrived at Chico Meadows, where a branch of Big Chico Creek ran through a lovely green meadow about three hundred acres in size. A number of springs along the edge supplied the stream with even more water. The Woodsum brothers had a lumber mill located there that at one time employed from twenty-six to thirty men and would crank out about twenty thousand feet of lumber per day. The loud puffing of the huge steam engine and its shrill whistle—screaming morning, noon and night—reminded the residents of the little hamlet, consisting of a boardinghouse and some cabins, that although the place was used as a summer resort for some, there was still much work being done.[26]

The Woodsum brothers operated another lumber mill lower on the Humboldt Road, possibly near Wakefield's. That mill was originally built by Jo Morrill around 1864 but was purchased by the Woodsums in about 1866.[27] The Woodsum brothers later sold the upper mill to Allen, Taylor and Holbrook. In those days, it was common for mill ownership to change hands frequently.

Late in this decade, C.F. Ellsworth began to establish himself as a major lumberman in the area. He located his portable sawmill near Wakefield's, later referred to as the Forest Mill, and began cutting up to ten thousand feet per day.[28] He also operated the Comet Mill, located about twenty miles from Chico, and produced about eighteen thousand shingles per day. Evidence suggests that it was sometime around the turn of the decade that Ellsworth built the Empire Mill, located in the vicinity of the McGann place. It averaged thirty-six thousand feet per day.[29]

What about gold? Although the initial rush had quieted down somewhat, there was still plenty of the precious yellow material waiting to be found in the foothills of Butte County, and the auriferous gravels of the West Branch of Butte Creek were only a couple of miles from the road, near McDonald's. In the previous decade, it was reported that a whopping lump of gold weighing twenty-nine pounds and nine ounces was taken from a claim in this locality. It was estimated that the "monster chunk" contained only about four ounces of quartz.[30] In 1866, Portuguese Point, a stretch of ground along this same waterway, gave up one nugget weighing about fourteen ounces—still not too shabby.[31]

A Brutal Killing in the Desert

The year 1865 was a time of heightened conflict between the white settlers and the natives of the Black Rock Desert, and the new road from Chico to Idaho and the fork to the Humboldt mining area were caught right

1860s: The Road to the Mines

in the middle of it. In fact, the sudden increase in traffic from Chico to the distant mines likely triggered some of the violent episodes the desert witnessed that year.

It should be noted that when the white explorers and early settlers first arrived in the Black Rock region, relations with the indigenous people were fairly amicable. However, after massive numbers of immigrants began to pour into the area, it was not long before the natives realized that available game was disappearing and grass for their own stock was being destroyed by the countless animals the newcomers brought with them. Most of the immigrants viewed the land as open and free for the taking and thought local Indians had no property rights. Of course, the Indians didn't see it that way, and many looked at the new settlers as ruthless invaders. Not only were they being squeezed out of their own homeland, but indiscriminate killing of Indians by whites also prompted some bands to take revenge in a most furious way.

The news reported deadly incidents in this general area throughout 1865, as the inhabitants of the land endured a series of attacks and reprisals. Both white settlers and Indians were murdered; stock was stolen, run off or killed; and property was destroyed.[32] Early in 1865, hostile Indians were blamed in

Indians attacking cowboys in Frederic Remington's 1903 painting (original in color) *Fight for the Waterhole. Courtesy of the Museum of Fine Arts, Houston, the Hogg Brothers Collection, gift of Miss Ima Hogg.*

the killing of one white man at Wall Springs. Later, three occupants of the Granite Creek Station (a supply stop near today's town of Gerlach, Nevada) were killed by Indians.[33] The four murders occurred along the road that was used by travelers on the way from Chico.[34]

Later that year, a man from Dogtown, now known as Magalia (located near Chico), was also killed by Indians. Newspapers from Chico and Unionville, Nevada, reported the gruesome incident. The following statement was made by a man named A.T. Clark, who was hauling freight with several others from Chico to the Humboldt mining area. The quote was published in the November 18, 1865 *Humboldt Register*, a newspaper located in Unionville:

> *I was coming from Chico to Star City with four teams: three of them mine, one of them J.W. Bellew's. At Granite Creek one of my teamsters took sick. I had to double wagons, and as I could not travel as fast as formerly, Bellew went ahead till we got to Rabit [sic] Hole, which I reached about 11 o'clock p.m. on Friday, Nov. 3. Found no hay. We rested till next day, 10 a.m. The station keeper told us that he was expecting a load of hay from the river. Bellew said he would drive on, and when he met the hay he would get some of it, and stop at Cedar Station—13 miles from Rabit Hole.*
>
> *When I reached the summit, four and a half miles from Cedar Station, I saw Bellew about three miles ahead, and about one mile from the narrow defile close to Cedar Station—at this time the sun was about fifteen minutes high. When I got within two miles of the Station, I saw a smoke gathering in a kind of vapory cloud off to the right of the road, and supposed that Bellew had started a camp fire. Soon I saw flames very high; still thought it was Bellew.*
>
> *Kept on under this impression till I got within forty steps of the wagon, when I found that it was on fire. The wagon was almost consumed, and falling to pieces. It was loaded with butter, molasses, and whiskey, for Luff, of Star. The whiskey, melted butter, and molasses, were all running in streams down the road. Saw at once that it was the work of Indians. Found that they had taken off the wheel cattle and driven them away—retreating south over Antelope Mountain. I reached there about 8 o'clock p.m. I hurried past Cedar Station to Willow Station, five miles further, and roused the keeper; got him a horse from a teamster there, and started him to the river for assistance. This was about midnight. I staid [sic] there till daylight, then went back to the summit to see if I could see my teams. Found them all right. It was not long before men came from the river, and with them I went down to the burnt wagon—getting there about 8 a.m.—and found*

> *Bellew's wagon in this condition: The wagon and load completely burned to the ground; the wheel cattle gone; the remaining four yoke of cattle hitched to the tongue, which they had carried off, and grazing round in the brush.*
>
> *Found Bellew's body about one hundred yards from the wagon. He had run back towards us. We did not see him as we came along, as he laid on the right side of the road and we were on the left of our cattle, driving. We found him naked, shot with six or eight balls and as many arrows; body cut open, and entrails strewn over the ground, and other portions of the body subjected to all other disgusting mutilations practiced only by these savage monsters.*
>
> *We took a wagon sheet, wrapped the body up in it, and brought it to the Humboldt river. Procured a coffin, and had the body decently buried at Clark & Bell's, on the Humboldt, at 10 a.m., of the 8th.*
>
> *Bellew was a man of family: wife and six children to mourn his loss. They reside within three miles of Dog Town, Butte County, California.*

Although the military had been attempting to suppress the Indian rebellion for years, this particular attack, on an unarmed teamster, appears to have spurred a sense of urgency. (The news reported that, oddly enough, none of the freight haulers were carrying firearms.) A company of about twenty mounted soldiers from Dun Glen, a military post located about nine miles northeast of Mill City, Nevada, was called to pursue the Indians and serve justice. The soldiers, led by Lieutenant Penwell, employed a Paiute Indian leader named Captain Sou to act as their guide.[35] It was believed that Captain Sou assisted the military in ridding the country of renegade Indians because he felt they were threatening the destruction of the entire Paiute tribe at the hands of angry whites.

It was determined that the killing was the work of Black Rock Tom (also referred to as Captain Tom) and his band of renegade Indians. The outlaw raiders were one of several renegade bands who terrorized whites in the Black Rock region that year, although it's been suggested that it was Tom's band that was mostly responsible for the depredations along the Black Rock portion of the Chico road to the Humboldt mining area. If one was to believe the December 30, 1865 *Humboldt Register*, Black Rock Tom had the stuff to become legendary:

> *All hunters of Indians, who came to an engagement anywhere between this and Owyhee, and almost all parties attacked on that road, during the past season, remarked a white horse of extraordinary qualities, the rider*

of which seemed to take great pride in his efforts to "witch the world with noble horsemanship." The white horse was ever spoken of as a wonder of strength and fleetness. His rider, a stalwart Indian, delighted to dally just out of musket range from the white men, caricoling [sic] most provokingly, and darting off, occasionally, with the fleetness of the wind. The rider was "Black Rock Tom."

The news reported that after investigating the scene of Bellew's murder, Lieutenant Penwell sent a messenger back to Dun Glen to request reinforcements to aid in his pursuit of the guilty Indians. Consequently, another native guide, Piute Sam, and ten more soldiers were added to his force. The lieutenant and his men eventually located the renegades but found them firmly entrenched in a natural fortress of steep walls of stone on a mountain. (It's been suggested that this battle took place at a location some fifteen or twenty miles southwest of Summit Lake.) After failing to dislodge the large band of well-protected Indians, the soldiers abandoned the attack and returned to Dun Glen. Historical accounts disagree on the true number of casualties on either side, but suffice it to say, they were very small, if any at all.[36]

Shortly afterward, Lieutenant Osmer left Dun Glen for the general area where the renegades were last seen, taking with him a howitzer, sixty soldiers and a few citizens. Captain Sou and a small number of his warriors joined the hunting party. This time, the campaign was more successful for the pursuers, as they were in a place that was not nearly as well protected for the natives. Some of the plunder from Bellew's wagon was recovered at the scene. One soldier was killed and two were wounded, but the renegade band was decimated.[37] It is not clear how many Indians were actually killed, but it was likely somewhere around one hundred. A few of them managed to escape, however, including Black Rock Tom.

In January 1866, the last large organized group of Black Rock Indian raiders was found near the confluence of the Quinn River (referred to as Queen's River back then) and Fish Creek by a company from Dun Glen that was led by Captain Conrad and a company from Fort McDermitt (located near the east fork of the Quinn River, close to the Nevada-Oregon border) that was led by Lieutenant Duncan. The news reported that sixty soldiers, ten civilians and twelve friendly Paiutes participated in the final large-scale campaign waged against outlaw Indians still on the loose.

As the battle took place in the middle of winter, the bitterly cold conditions produced extreme hardships that everyone had to endure up to and during the fight. Early on, the expedition on horseback had to contend with blowing snow as the men made their way to the battleground. When they neared the renegade encampment on the night march, the Indian hunters had to stop short and dismount at 3:00 a.m., lest they be noticed by the enemy before the planned daylight raid. With the freezing temperatures dropping quickly, the men, who were already under considerable duress by that point, were compelled to form large circles on the snowy desert floor and run around in them to keep warm—telltale campfires were not allowed. The bizarre-looking scene lasted for three hours. Despite this extraordinary effort to save themselves, more than one-quarter of the men had frozen hands, feet or faces. Just before the battle began, dense clouds of frost formed, reducing visibility and forcing the soldiers to fight at short range, making them more susceptible to the bow and arrow. When it was all over, the cavalry prevailed once again. Although some white men were wounded, none were killed. The same could not be said for the renegade group, which lost more than thirty-five members. The threat that the Indian uprising posed to settlers in this particular area was dampened considerably with the elimination of these warriors in the harsh conditions of the Black Rock Desert in January.[38]

Black Rock Tom was not present during this last event because he had already turned himself in at Big Meadows, Nevada (referred to as Lovelock today), in hopes of forming some kind of treaty. (The white horse was not with him.) He was eventually taken prisoner by Captain Street, who handed him over to some of his men, specifically instructing them to not allow the captured Indian to escape. When Black Rock Tom tried to do just that, he didn't get very far. Musket balls stopped him dead in his tracks.[39]

THE "MAD" RUSH FOR BLACK ROCK SILVER

Early in 1866, it was reported that a long-lost silver ledge had been rediscovered in Black Rock Range, Nevada, which just happened to be near the Chico to Idaho stage road. Another mineral rush was on. The *Chico Courant* followed the events closely, and several of Chico's most prominent citizens took part in the frenzy that resulted from this purported bonanza. From the time the ledge was first discovered to when the silver rush came to a sudden end, the events that unfolded had twists and turns that make it possibly one of the strangest stories ever told about a lost mine.

It all began back in 1849, when a man called James Hardin accidentally stumbled across what would become known afterward as the Hardin ledge. Hardin was the member of a wagon train traveling along the Applegate-Lassen Emigrant Trail. When the party reached the southern portion of the Black Rock Range, which extended northward from the desert's namesake butte, Hardin and at least one other man left the train for a time and went hunting for game along the western slope of the range. They came upon a small ravine and noticed some shiny material on the bottom. (Andrew Hardin, a nephew of James, recalled that his uncle later said to him that there was about a wagonload of it.)

The story goes that the men assumed it was probably lead, so they collected some samples and brought the rock specimens back to camp to fashion into bullets, although it is not certain that was ever accomplished. Nonetheless, James Hardin kept some of the material and brought it to Petaluma, California, where he settled. Sometime afterward, the rock was assayed and found to be high in silver content. So, in 1858, James Hardin and a party of men organized an expedition and went to the Black Rock Desert to relocate the silver ledge. Unfortunately, the search failed to produce any of the metallic substance because either the country had changed considerably or Hardin simply forgot where it was located. Hardin and some others came back the next year, and some say the year after that, but with no more success.

Peter Lassen, who developed the Lassen Emigrant Trail (sharing a section of Applegate's route that passed through the Black Rock Desert), also searched for this lost silver lode. Lassen is regarded as one of the most iconic figures in Northern California history. The old pioneer will not soon be forgotten around these parts. Today, there are countless places in Northern California named after him, including Lassen County, Lassen Peak, Lassen Park, Lassen National Forest, Lassen College, Lassen Avenue and Lassen Steakhouse. The list goes on.

It just so happened that Peter Lassen accompanied John Bidwell on the expedition to retrieve the horses that were stolen near Sutter's Fort back in 1843. It was on this trip that Lassen first saw his future piece of paradise, too, and in 1844, he received a land grant for Rancho Bosquejo, a chunk of ground more than twenty-two thousand acres in size, located where the town of Vina is today. Unfortunately, he did not keep the rancho for long, selling the last part of it in 1852 and eventually settling in Honey Lake Valley.

Like many men in those days, Peter Lassen was caught up in the excitement of trying to make a fortune through prospecting. While he was

1860s: The Road to the Mines

Sketch of Peter Lassen. *From Gilbert's 1882 work* History of California from 1513 to 1850.

living in Honey Lake Valley, reports of a rich silver deposit in the Black Rock country inspired him to go out to see if he could locate it. In April 1859, he left with Lemericus Wyatt and Edward Clapper for the Black Rock Desert. The plan was to rendezvous with a Captain Weatherlow and three other men at a specified place near the prospecting site. Even though they left two days before Lassen's party, for some reason, Weatherlow's group was not there when Lassen and company arrived, so Lassen and his companions camped in a small canyon nearby. It was reported that while they were staying at this place, the three men were ambushed from the ridge above by an unknown sniper. Lassen and Clapper were shot and killed. Wyatt made a miraculous escape.

Who killed Peter Lassen, and why, remains a mystery. Although Indians were originally thought to have been responsible, there was evidence suggesting that a white man, or men, may have actually killed the well-liked pioneer who was sometimes affectionately referred to as Uncle Pete. Many theories surfaced, some even implicating Wyatt or Weatherlow.

After Wyatt managed to make it back to Honey Lake Valley to tell of his ordeal, a party went out to the scene and buried the bodies of Lassen and Clapper where they were found. Later that year, Lassen's body was retrieved and brought back to be laid to rest in Honey Lake Valley. Clapper's was left where it was. The ever-changing landscape revealed some of Clapper's remains for desert recreationalists to discover in May 1990. The bones from Lassen's prospecting companion were then reburied in a grave not far from the old trailblazer's.

It's been well over one hundred years and we seem no closer to solving the puzzling death of one of our most famous and beloved historical figures than we ever were. The mystery will likely never be solved.

The enthusiasm in searching for the lost silver ledge slowed over the next few years, at least partly because of intermittent Indian hostilities. Nonetheless, a small number of men still persisted in looking.

Then, in January 1866, the situation suddenly changed. Word got out that the elusive Hardin ledge had finally been rediscovered as well as other potentially productive ledges. (The first ledge was actually said to be discovered in the fall of 1865.) Being relatively close, the Susanville area was particularly excited about the new discoveries, and some of its citizens wasted no time going to get in on the action and spread the word.[40] As more ledges were found—some reported to be up to one hundred feet wide and several miles long[41]—prospectors began to swarm into the region from all over.[42]

Some amazing stories were reported by the papers, especially in regard to the estimated value of the ores, often getting these figures from overly exuberant miners. The February 17, 1866 *Chico Courant* published:

> *There is considerable excitement in and about Susanville and the adjacent country in reference to the richness of the mines lately discovered at Black Rock. A person informs us, and we have no reason to doubt his veracity, though it is a large thing to swallow, that the people out there are just frying the silver out of the rock taken from the ledges, in spoons, ladles, kettles and even frying pans....*

The March 24, 1866 *Humboldt Register* reported:

> BLACKROCK *is all the go now. Thursday fore-noon a snow storm was on, which turned, about meridian, to rain; but it did not deter a number of prospectors from setting out for the new Dorado. When you see a man sitting in front of a roll of blankets and frying-pan, and behind a Henry rifle, you need not ask him where he is going—he's 'going to Blackrock—or burst.'*

However, from the beginning of the rush to the end, various tests on the Black Rock ores yielded differing results. Some indicated fabulous returns. Others showed nothing at all. While quite a few people were skeptical from the start, many were quickly caught up in the excitement about the riches that the material could potentially produce. The problem was that the mostly black (other colors were sometimes reported) waxy-looking ore, which was said to resemble the character of the material coming from the rich Owyhee mines in southwestern Idaho,[43] was considered atypical, and it was reported that very few people knew how to extract the silver from it. When assayers from Unionville tested it early on, they could find but a trace of silver. Later, it was reported that reputable assayers from various cities, including San Francisco, determined it contained no silver at all.[44]

1860s: The Road to the Mines

Then there was Professor Charles Isenbeck, an assayer and copper smelter from Genesee Valley, Plumas County (adjacent to and northeast of Butte County), California. In early 1866, Isenbeck declared Black Rock an immensely rich discovery,[45] defying the many experts who determined just the opposite. The professor's credentials: he was reported to be a graduate of Freiberg Institute in Germany, where a university that specializes in mining and technology is still located today. The silver-tongued (pun intended) metallurgist managed to convince enough people that he was the only one who really understood the extremely rebellious character of the Black Rock ore, with the silver existing in a chloride state that puzzled even the most experienced assayers most of the time.[46] Isenbeck claimed that he found not only silver in the material but also quantities of gold.[47]

Despite the conflicting reports on the true value of the ores, many people from nearby localities, particularly the Susanville area, were willing to jump right in on the action and stake their claims. By early spring, prospectors were locating ledges and homes were being built in anticipation of the big strike that seemed to some like almost a sure thing. The town of Chico was getting caught up in the excitement, too, with expectations of a big boost to the economy from providing supplies for the prospectors and the transportation of bullion over the Chico and Humboldt Wagon Road.[48] The *Chico Courant* kept track of the events in the Black Rock country, often citing other newspapers that were closer to the action, such as Susanville's *Sage Brush*, Unionville's *Humboldt Register* or Washoe City's *Eastern Slope*. To entice the local residents even more, people were coming from the Black Rock region to Chico and bringing promising news and samples of silver worked from the desert mines. This included men such as Judge Harvey of Susanville,[49] who was one of the first on the scene when the rush of 1866 began. One man in particular, J.C. Martin, a Chico attorney who owned some "feet," expressed great confidence in the wealth held in the Black Rock ores.[50] Mr. Martin was soon to play a significant role in getting the town of Chico involved in the Black Rock mineral rush.

In March 1866, it was reported that Isenbeck supervised the working of three tons of Judge Harvey's Black Rock ore at Torrey's Mill, located in the vicinity of Unionville, and determined that the process needed to be improved. Because of uncertainty early on, people from the Unionville area were hesitant to process any more ore from the Black Rock region.[51] However, people in Washoe Valley, located near the Comestock Lode, appeared to be more responsive. Arrangements were made in late spring to bring some one thousand pounds of the material to Dall's Mill, located in

Black Rock, the desert's namesake, is located at the southern end of the Black Rock Range. *Photo by author.*

Franktown (near Washoe City, about twenty miles south of today's Reno, on old US 395). The result was $126 to the ton, which was satisfying news for the people of Susanville. Therefore, plans were made to haul thirty to forty more tons to the mill to put any more questioning to rest.[52] These results were even more encouraging, so a mining company that was previously formed in Chico could now work the Black Rock mines with more confidence. (A lack of records suggest that this was probably not an incorporated company at the time but instead a loosely organized group of individuals with a common interest in mining, frequently referred to in the news as the "Chico company.") Letters coming to Chico were reassuring, suggesting that test results ranged anywhere from $200 to an amazing $6,000 per ton.[53]

Despite inhospitable conditions, things were looking quite promising for the Black Rock miners. The August 18, 1866 *Chico Courant* quoted the *Eastern Slope*:

> *The region around the mines is described to be most desolate; indeed, it is difficult to imagine why such a country was created, unless those cheerless wastes were meant as hiding places for treasure. The Black Rockers are*

described as a peculiar people. They have from three to eight thousand feet of ground each; feel certain they have a good thing; are sure they have treasure enough to build a Railroad, with silver rails, to Chico and Vallejo—which, by the way, is where nature intended the Railroad should be built—pay the national debt; and have enough left to buy Ireland for the Fenians and move it over to "Ameriky."

By September, two settlements were well established in the region—one at Double Springs, sometimes called Spring City (today referred to as the Double Hot Springs), and another at Hardin City, sometimes called Hardinville or Ram's Horn. Each had a post office.[54] At the time, Double Springs was reported to have half a dozen houses. Hardin City was made up of fifteen well-built houses, as well as grocery and liquor stores, butcher shops and a stable. A restaurant was started, and one white woman resided there. Plans were being made to transport an ore-crushing mill to the mining district. The mill was purchased from Virginia City by Evans and Harvey, residents of Honey Lake Valley.[55]

In October, the Chico news reported that J.C. Martin, having staked his claim in the Black Rock region, was returning to Chico to practice law once again. The paper joked that, measured in feet, the attorney was now worth millions of dollars.[56]

Nonetheless, the Black Rock mines remained a mystery. No one knew for sure whether they would prove to be a boom or a bust. The November 20, 1866 *Marysville Daily Appeal* pretty much summed it up: "The Black Rock region is attracting much attention at present, and is either the biggest thing or the biggest 'bilk' in all creation. Judging from the appearance of the rock it would seem to be the latter, but judging from facts and figures it is as near the former as Washoe, if not nearer."

By December, it was reported that the new mill at Hardin City was operating, and people were anxiously awaiting the results from the first experimentation in hopes of dispelling any more uncertainty.[57] However, they would have to wait. There were problems with the apparatus and material for amalgamation.[58]

The following month, the *Courant* reported that Mr. Martin had forwarded some Black Rock ore specimens to John Bidwell (a member of the Chico mining company) while the congressman was in Washington, D.C., and Bidwell then had the rock tested by the most highly qualified metallurgists and mineralogists in Europe. After the results determined the ore to be very rich, plans were made to reorganize the mining company on a more permanent basis. The Chico newspaper was further informed that the Mineralogical Institute at Freiberg made a proposition for an interest in the new company.[59] Now, things were really looking up for the Chico prospectors.

By April, more news stories of fantastic results coming from the Black Rock ores were surfacing, with one piece suggesting a value possibly around a whopping $9,000 per ton.[60] Professor Isenbeck ran a number of tests on various ledges for the Chico company and noted that not all of the ore from this desert area was troublesome to work. He claimed the green silver class of ore, for instance, was easy to deal with and still yielded at a rate of $238 to the ton,[61] a highly respectable amount.

With all of this promising news, the April 12, 1867 *Chico Courant* was again optimistic that the silver rush in Black Rock was going to create a substantial boon to its economy: "There will be a great rush to Black Rock, from Virginia City, the coming spring—so we are informed, and the prospect is that flourishing times are ahead. Chico is the natural point from which the Black Rock supplies will be procured, and the prospect of a huge trade, the coming summer, will cause our merchants to enlarge their stocks."

In June, it was revealed that the Chico company had extensive mines in the Black Rock region, and Mr. Isenbeck was still testing material from there in the interests of said company.[62] A reporter for the *Courant* wrote that he had seen the working test of three pounds of rock under the direction of the professor, applying what was referred to as the "bake pan process," which created a piece of amalgam as large as an English walnut. The following day, Isenbeck showed off a button of gold weighing four pennyweights and a vial full of chloride of silver that he formed from the amalgam. The reporter wrote that the three pounds of rock produced at a rate of nearly $4,000 to the ton. Some of the black wax was also worked the previous week by the professor and supposedly produced at a rate of $4 or $5 to the pound. Three Chico citizens, W.H. Duren, Thomas McFadden and Frank Johnson, left for the Black Rock with Isenbeck to thoroughly establish the value of the mines.[63] Unfortunately, in July, the mill that was supposed to be running by then was still unfit for work, forcing them to continue testing with the bake pan process.[64]

It was evident that the Chico company was sold on Isenbeck. On the other hand, the people from Unionville were never keen on the professor and his claims and did not hesitate to offer their opinions on the matter. The July 13, 1867 *Humboldt Register* had this to say:

Isenbeck.—This prince of humbugs is again on his way out to Black Rock, with a fresh installment of victims to insanity. We might have some sympathy for these people were they imposed upon by a man of ordinary intelligence, who was more knave than fool, and would in that case advise them to suspend him by the neck to the overhanging croppings [sic] of some one of his many rich quartz ledges in that district, but as it is, we feel no sympathy for them. If intelligent men will allow themselves to be humbugged from year to year by a creature who ought to be the inmate of a lunatic asylum, they of course have a perfect right to do so; but let them cease blowing through public journals of the riches of that section on the bare say-so of Isenbeck, for in this they deceive others who have not the means of judging of the amount of credibility that should be given to his sage opinions, but are left to a costly experience in time and money before learning how completely they have been sold.

In August, W.H. Duren and Professor Isenbeck were back in Chico, bringing with them the most flattering reports from Black Rock. They reported that some thirty or forty tons of ore were sent to Virginia City and that Mr. Isenbeck was on his way to assist in the working.[65]

In early September, the anticipation was growing. Frank Johnson came from Washoe to Chico, bringing more encouraging news and informing the locals that eight different ledges from the Black Rock area were worked there—not one yielded less than $200 per ton. The Chico-based miner predicted that within two months, three different mills would be in operating condition at Black Rock. It was felt that the tests made at Dall's Mill had shown beyond a doubt "that the mines are the richest in the world."[66]

A.C. Longmore of the Susanville *Sage Brush* visited Chico and said he assisted in the working of the rock at Dall's Mill. He indicated that this was the final test to determine whether the rock was rich or worthless. Under Isenbeck's supervision and in the presence of professional metallurgists, the results from different ledges produced values from $140 to $340 per ton. That was enough to convince everyone. The two other mills were ordered. Evans, Bass and Co., partners in the ownership of the Hardin City mill, agreed to hire Isenbeck at $1,000 per month.[67] The professor's future was looking mighty fine.

By then, the miners from Chico were getting serious too. On September 21, 1867, the Chico Gold and Silver Mining Company was incorporated for extracting gold, silver and other metals in the Hardin Mining District of Humboldt County, Nevada, and acquiring property as necessary to carry on the operation of the company. With a capital stock of $200,000, the principal place of business was in Chico, California. The stock consisted of two thousand shares at $100 each. John Bidwell, J.C. Mandeville, J.C. Martin, Thomas McFadden and Ira A. Wetherbee were assigned as the trustees to manage the concerns of the company for the first three months. At this time, eight other men, including the aforementioned W.H. Duren, F.F. Johnson and A.C. Longmore, were also identified as original investors in the formation of the company.[68] In October 1867, stock certificates were signed, entitling shareholders to a piece of the action. On the certificates, it can be seen that J.C. Martin was the secretary and John Bidwell was the president of the company.

W.H. Duren, one of the founders of the new mining company, was a justice of the peace and the established owner of a bookstore across from J.C. Martin's office. In October, with expectations of good times ahead, Duren left the town of Chico for Black Rock to establish a business and look after his interests in the mines.[69] Later that month, it was reported that several teams were being loaded with merchandise at Chico and were destined for Hardin City.[70] The wheels were in motion.

However, by mid-November, the optimism quickly began to wane when the Evans and Company mill at Hardin City, which was specially equipped to suit Isenbeck's process, was finally ready to crush the rock on a large scale. L. Bass, part owner, claimed that more than ten tons of Black Rock ore was worked at the mill but failed to produce a trace of gold or silver. Bass and

Chico Gold and Silver Mining Company stock certificate. J.C. Mandeville was an original investor in the wagon road too. *Courtesy of Holabird Western Americana Collections.*

1860s: The Road to the Mines

CHICO HOTEL—IRA. A. WETHERBEE, PROPRIETOR.
CHICO, BUTTE CO. CAL.

Ira A. Wetherbee, hotel owner, was an original investor in the Chico Gold and Silver Mining Company. *Courtesy of CSU, Chico, Meriam Library, Special Collections.*

Isenbeck were at odds and gave different stories to the press.[71] When the *Sage Brush* got wind of the unsuccessful attempt, Chico's own Frank Johnson produced a rather peculiar response. He told the newspaper not to worry because there was no effort made to acquire a large amount.[72]

Soon after, it was reported that J.B. Hiskey, the superintendent at Dall's Mill, was expected to go to Black Rock to help in the reduction of the ores. The *Sage Brush* was informed that the people from Dall's were so confident in its value that they were willing to purchase much more of the controversial material and to pay $100 per ton to have it delivered to their mill.[73]

Nonetheless, after that point, the *Courant* became mysteriously silent. The optimistic reporting the Chico paper had put out over the past two years suddenly came to an end. It appears the editor was starting to smell a rat.

The recent failure prompted the *Humboldt Register* to remind readers once more of the folly of following the likes of Isenbeck, whom the paper viewed as an imposter and lunatic. The Unionville news decided to do some homework and subsequently provided numerous pieces of evidence showing that the professor appeared to have quite a history of fraud before he even showed up in the Black Rock region. It republished a letter sent by a disgruntled citizen to the editor of the *Montgomery Pioneer* in 1864. (The town of Montgomery was located in Mono County, California.) The citizen claimed that Mr. Isenbeck deceived quite a few people in that town with his promises of riches contained in the Montgomery rock, injuring one person in particular who provided the cash to build an expensive smelting furnace that ultimately proved useless. Phony bars of silver were imported to promote the deception. The scheme seemed similar to the Black Rock situation. The November 30, 1867 *Humboldt Register* wrote that it republished the 1864 letter to the *Pioneer* "for the especial benefit of those moon-struck individuals of large faith who are still following the *ignis fatuus* of Blackrock and Isenbeck into the dismal swamp of costly experience."

Nonetheless, some Black Rockers still held out hope. In December, the *Humboldt Register* reported that two runs of five tons each were made at the newly erected Atchison Mill (located north of the Evans and Company Mill at Hardin City)[74] with the same disappointing result.[75] In one last effort, there were a few more attempts, but again, no luck. By the end of January the following year, pretty much all hope was lost, and few people remained in the Black Rock region.[76] In April, it was reported that the Black Rock prospectors had totally abandoned the area.[77]

In 1869, Rossiter W. Raymond, special commissioner of mining statistics, Treasury Department, wrote a rather scathing report on the matter on page 120 of his book titled *Mineral Resources of the States and Territories West of the Rocky Mountains*. (On the following page, he noted that the Black Rock District was actually made of several districts, including the Hardin and High Rock, where the Chico company made claims.) This is what Raymond had to say:

> *Black Rock district.—This district, comprising a large portion of the northwestern quarter of Humboldt county, has been the scene of hopes as wild and disappointments as overwhelming as any recorded in the history of American mines. As early as 1859 the notice of acute, but ignorant observers was attracted by a dark-colored rock, occurring in heavy masses in that region, about a hundred miles from Unionville. It was a bituminous clay, and the associated rocks were almost without exception volcanic, giving no encouragement for the discovery of precious metals. But the waxy texture of the clay, doubtless being compared to that of the rich silver ore known*

> as horn-silver, (chloride of silver,) was considered a "good indication," and it was not long before the story found credence that a new ore of silver had been discovered in the "black wax" of Humboldt county. Respectable assayers in the Pacific States, and, to my knowledge, also in New York, flatly contradicted the popular delusion. But the Black Rock people had an assayer of their own—a man by the name of Isenbeck—who claimed that no one but himself could extract the silver from these peculiar ores. He worked by what he called the Freiberg process, and made use of a peculiar flux. It seems strange that intelligent men could believe such trash. Of course Mr. Isenbeck's secret flux contained a compound of silver. Six or seven years passed away in experiments and explorations. The people of the Pacific coast were the victims far more than eastern capitalists. They wanted to keep the good thing to themselves. At last, in 1867, Mr. Isenbeck announced that he was ready to work the rock on a large scale, and 13 tons were hauled for him from different ledges to Dall's mill, in Washoe county. The result announced was $70 to $400 per ton. A renewed excitement was the consequence. A mill was built in the Black Rock country, to be managed by Isenbeck. Two others were put in active preparation. But Mr. Isenbeck could not afford to use his flux on a large scale; and, before operations commenced, he disappeared from the public eye. The Black Rock miners, who had shown for more than six years a grim determination and perseverance worthy of respect, though they had been credulous as children of the stories of this charlatan, abandoned their mines in despair. Houses, mills, everything was left as it stood, and in the summer of 1868 there was not a human being in the district. Even thieves would not go there to steal the abandoned property. An expedition sent to the region by Mr. Clarence King confirmed the opinion of all scientific men from the beginning, that "Black Rock was a swindle."

Unsurprisingly, soon after the Atchison Mill failures, the blame game began to surface. Probably in defense of the choice made by its locals, the *Chico Courant* wondered why Isenbeck was shouldering all of the blame. The paper felt that the attention should have been directed at J.B. Hiskey, the superintendent of the Washoe mill who worked much of the ore. Hiskey consistently produced great results, while promoting the richness of Black Rock material until the very end. The *Courant* even went so far as to accuse the Dall's Mill superintendent of salting the ore.[78]

What about Hiskey? Why was he getting such great results? Unlike Isenbeck, the mill superintendent did not appear to have a history of

No luck finding any silver? No problem. You can always look for some pretty rocks nearby. *Photo by author.*

dishonesty, and his intentions were generally not questioned, despite the *Courant*'s accusations. Many felt he was probably duped by Isenbeck like everyone else.[79] But if Isenbeck did deceive him, how could it have been done with such massive amounts of rock, and how did Hiskey continue to get such great results when Isenbeck wasn't even around? It's been suggested by one historian that Hiskey was most likely finding silver because his mill was crushing the Black Rock ore with batteries and pans that were not thoroughly cleaned after working truly rich ores from the Comstock mines and that the alkali dust of the Black Rock ore was breaking the Comstock silver loose. But, in reality, no one knows for sure. Hiskey's role remains a mystery today.

Despite the failure of the black wax to produce anything of value, is there still a legitimate silver ledge out there waiting for someone to rediscover it after being lost for over 150 years? Who knows? James Hardin certainly thought it was worth going back to look. (Note that he found something shiny that did not sound much like the black waxy clay that created the mad rush of the 1860s.) In only a few moments, violent desert thunderstorms can tear open a mountainside and expose minerals that were hidden for hundreds, or even thousands, of years. Just as quickly, though, these cloud bursts can bury them again for many more years.

Maybe you'd be interested in trying to locate Hardin's lost silver ledge. It could be just underneath the surface, waiting for a gully washer to uncover it once more for some lucky prospector to find. So, if you don't mind hot days, cold nights and unpredictable winds; sharing your blood with a few mosquitoes, gnats and ticks; and it's not too much a bother to sidestep a rattlesnake or two, then the Black Rock Desert just might be the place for you.

STAGE ROBBERY NEAR THE BIG SUMMIT

Indians weren't the only dangerous humans people had to be on the lookout for while riding the stage over the road that went from Chico to the distant mining regions. Passing through isolated sections with valuables on board made travelers prime targets for stage robbers, commonly referred to as highwaymen. On an early Monday morning in late August 1866, a robbery on Bidwell's new thoroughfare took place near the Big Summit. Two bandits stopped the stage with the driver and five passengers on board. Passengers O'Rourke, Johnson, Bell and LeCount were coming from Idaho. Alex Young (Sandy), a butcher with the firm Kampf and Young, of Chico, had been to Susanville to buy some cattle. The September 1, 1866 *Chico Courant* read:

> *At the time the Stage was stopped the passengers were asleep, and it appears they did not get fairly woke up until the affair was over, or they would not have suffered themselves to be robbed so easily. Sandy lost $650, gold coin; O'Rourke $600, coin and a watch valued at $250, and two revolvers; Johnson lost $240, coin; Bell lost a revolver and gold watch and LeCount lost $25. One of the men had $1500 in his blankets, which he saved. The driver said if he had been armed he could have winged both of the birds, as one of them appeared green at the business, and trembled like an aspen leaf. They wanted to take the driver's watch; Jehu objected, and they did not persist. Sandy came a short distance with the Stage and went back, got the assistance of Ike Dye, an old Indian Hunter; struck the trail of the robbers; found were [sic] they burried [sic] their tools with which they opened W.F. & Co's treasure box; tools were recognizing [sic] as coming from a shop in Indian Valley; found the tracks of the robbers, fresh; at last accounts were*

Hi Good (*left*) and Sandy Young fought in many Indian battles and joined numerous posses together. In this photo, they appear to be posing in a gesture of solidarity. *Courtesy of CSU, Chico, Meriam Library, Special Collections.*

near the scoundrels, and if either Ike or Sandy draws bead on one of them there will be a dead robber in the woods. Ike and Sandy won't take any prisoners for the State to bother with. Both know the mountains as well as a man knows his garden patch, and we may expect to hear that these fellows have done their last job of robbing.

What the paper failed to mention was that Sandy Young was quite the Indian hunter himself. In fact, he and the aforementioned Hi Good were the best of friends and often worked together in raids on the local native population and in vigilante groups chasing white outlaws. (Sandy was the one who executed the Indian boy who murdered Hi Good, referred to earlier.) However, it is not known whether Sandy was ever able to exact his revenge on the robbers who took his money on that summer morning in 1866, or if the criminals were even apprehended.

Whatever the case, Sandy got a chance to take out his frustration on some other robbers who made the mistake of robbing a stage just below Magalia on the road from Oroville to Susanville (Humbug Road) the following year. One of the robbery victims was named A.T. Clark, from Chico Landing, and was very likely the same person who reported the Bellew killing to the *Humboldt Register* a couple of years before. The three robbers draped themselves in flour sacks with holes cut out for the eyes and mouths.[80] Despite their well-conceived cover clothes, Mr. Clark, while crossing over the mountains with a load of freight a short time later, reported that he thought he recognized one of the robbers buying supplies at Dye's ranch, located a few miles east of the Big Summit on the Chico and Humboldt Wagon Road. It appears the robber suspected that he was recognized, so he found his two partners nearby and they made haste to evade pursuit. Unfortunately for them, Hi Good, Sandy Young and three others were notified and were soon hot on their trail. After a two-day chase, the "scoundrels" were apprehended. One of the highwaymen tried to escape, but it was reported that Sandy Young fired at him and took him down. The man eventually succumbed to his mortal wound.[81] Sandy got his man, but he probably wasn't the one he wanted most.

Tollgate Violators, Human and Otherwise

Just because there were tollgates on the road, that didn't mean that everyone felt they should have to pay. In November 1869, two parties were prosecuted in Justice Hallet's court for failing to compensate the owners of the Chico and Humboldt Wagon Road for using their highway. Bidwell and company were eventually able to recover the whole sum sued for (seventy dollars), but it took two juries to come to an agreement on the amount. Apparently, the defendants felt that one way to avoid paying the toll was to simply operate between gates.[82]

When it came to paying tolls, humans weren't the only ones who felt they were permitted to skirt the law. The following incident occurred at the first tollgate out of Chico, located at the site that was later to be known as the Fourteen-Mile House. The tongue-in-cheek clipping was published in the June 14, 1867 *Chico Courant* and showed that, despite the fear that this beast could strike into the hearts of even the bravest of men, there was still room to make light of some encounters: "Last week, a huge grizzly bear came up to the toll-gate, at Cement Springs, about 12 miles from Chico, on the Idaho road, and as the gate-keeper refused to let him pass without the usual toll, bruin quietly marched round the gate, and turning his head with a grin at the astonished gate-keeper, leisurely trotted on up the road."

They Knew How to Party at Camp Jones

During the 1860s, Camp Jones, also referred to as Jonesville, appeared to keep the local news apprised of its happenings more than any other settlement along the stretch between Chico and Prattville. Though it was isolated in the mountains east of Chico, the lively little community was not devoid of good entertainment, at least not during the summer of 1869. Forty people were present for the Fourth of July holiday, which was celebrated with a dazzling display of fireworks that probably wouldn't even be legal in today's wildfire-conscious society. The July 10, 1869 *Northern Enterprise* printed the story, which was provided by a "Jonesvillian" correspondent:

> *The day passed away silently and without other demonstration than preparation for the evening. Soon after dark a large fire-cracker, by its report, announced the commencement of the ceremony. All the inhabitants for a mile around gathered in. Roman candles were touched off and pinwheels went spinning through the air, lighting up the whole surrounding scenery. We had a jolly good time, and every heart and hand was engaged. An orator was then called for, but none could be found in our midst. It was*

a disappointment, but we could not help it. After giving three cheers for the Fourth of July, three cheers for the ladies present, and three cheers for Jonesville, the inhabitants retired, some to pop corn, some to eat refreshments and others to bed. Hurrah for the 4th of July and Camp Jones.

Less than two weeks later, a costume party created some awkward moments that were thoroughly enjoyed by all. The July 24, 1869 *Northern Enterprise* printed this story:

On Friday evening, the 15th of July, a grand masquerade ball was given at Jonesville. Quite a number of our Chicoites were present as invited guests, and describe the occasion as one of the most pleasant, jolly and happy parties they had ever known. Some 40 persons were present, and up to the time (12 o'clock P.M.) when the masks were removed, there prevailed an entire ignorance of the identity of each other present. Single gentlemen in a state of blissful ignorance, were paying earnest devoirs to married ladies, and married ladies deeming their perceptive powers equal to the occasion, and declaring that no masked husband could disguise himself beyond her ability to discern, were found leaning "familiarly, confidingly, lovingly," upon the arm of the "stranger." The costumes were well designed, and in marked appropriateness established the characters sought to be represented. Kings and queens, lords and ladies, Scottish chief and peasant, fairies, sprites and gipsies [sic] *were present, and when to the designating costume was added the quaint manners and customs of the olden time as appropriate to the respective characters taken, it gave to the scene and occasion an unrestrained freedom which made the heart light with joy, and the ball to resound with peals of merry laughter. When the hour for supper came, and all stood unmasked, and the "mistakes of the evening" became apparent, then no sense of decorum or assumption of gravity was equal to the restraint of the wild boisterous laughter which came of the recollection of* queer things done and *funny things* said.

2
1870s

A Postal Route Established

Overview

As to be expected, the road underwent significant changes over the course of the 1870s. Land development was on the rise.

In 1881, the news reported that Hog Springs was formerly the site of several rickety old buildings, which were loosely referred to as a saloon and hotel.[83] This suggests that at some time in the 1870s, habitable structures, albeit of questionable integrity, were there to accommodate road travelers.

A way station, called the Ten-Mile House, appeared to first receive attention in the news during this decade. John H. Perkins owned the public house in the early part of the decade. Perkins wasn't always known to be a good host, however, according to S.S. Jud, a teamster. Jud, who already had a history of conflict with Perkins, made the mistake one day of stopping by the Ten-Mile building and was subsequently rewarded with a severe beating before getting shot at by the proprietor. Perkins was arrested and went to trial over the offense.[84] Later in the decade, "old man" Cox owned and operated the Ten-Mile House for a while before Mrs. Ferris managed the place around 1876. At that time, the news reported that the water for the Ten-Mile House had to be hauled up from a nearby ravine, and travelers who watered their teams there were asked to pay a fee.[85] Late in the decade, James McVey took over the place.[86]

In the early part of the decade, David Craig and family moved into the tollhouse location (referred to as the Fourteen-Mile House sometime

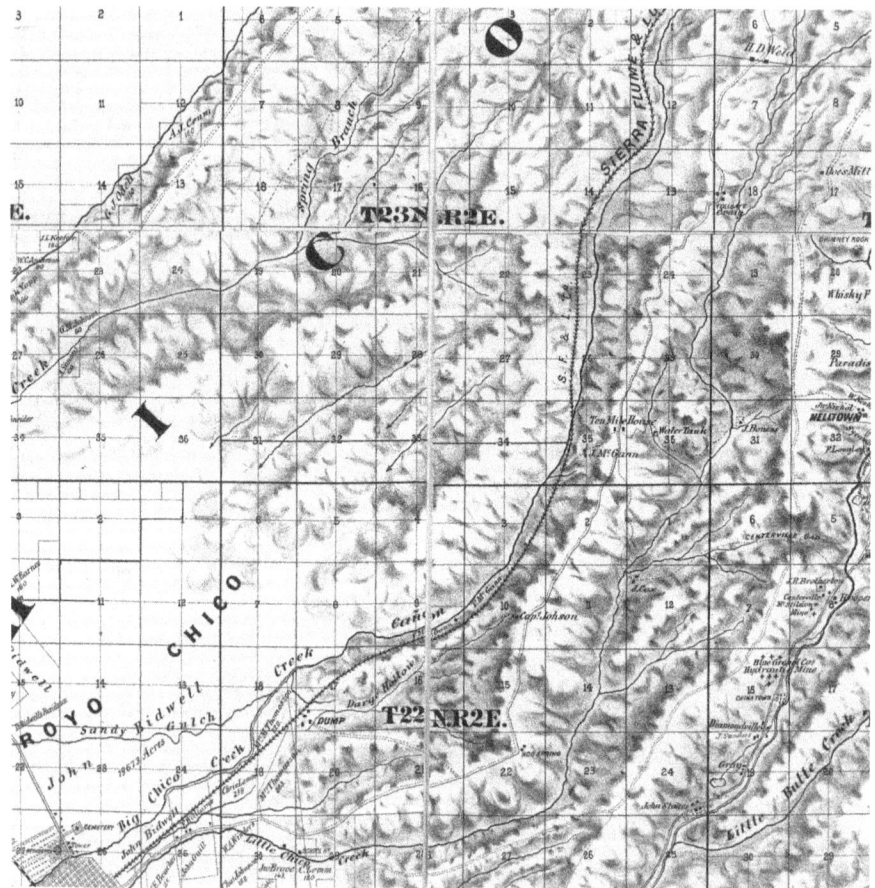

Lower third of the Butte County portion of Chico and Humboldt Wagon Road, showing where it leaves Chico and passes the Ten-Mile House and Weld's. From *Official Map of the County of Butte, California, 1877*, compiled by James McGann. *Courtesy of Library of Congress.*

later), which was known to provide a good place to wash up and get served a nice breakfast, although meals were offered just about any time.[87] Late in the decade, a new tollhouse was erected one mile up the road from the Fourteen-Mile House.[88]

During the first part of the decade, Elias Findley still had the place about sixteen miles from Chico. In 1873, he purchased the nearby Dashaway Mill from Aldersley and McCormick. The plant supplied general lumber, shakes and posts.[89] Around the mid-1870s, Mr. and Mrs. Weld took over Findley's residence. The couple spent some time improving the stop along the road. They catered to road travelers and sportsmen and offered good stabling

1870s: A Postal Route Established

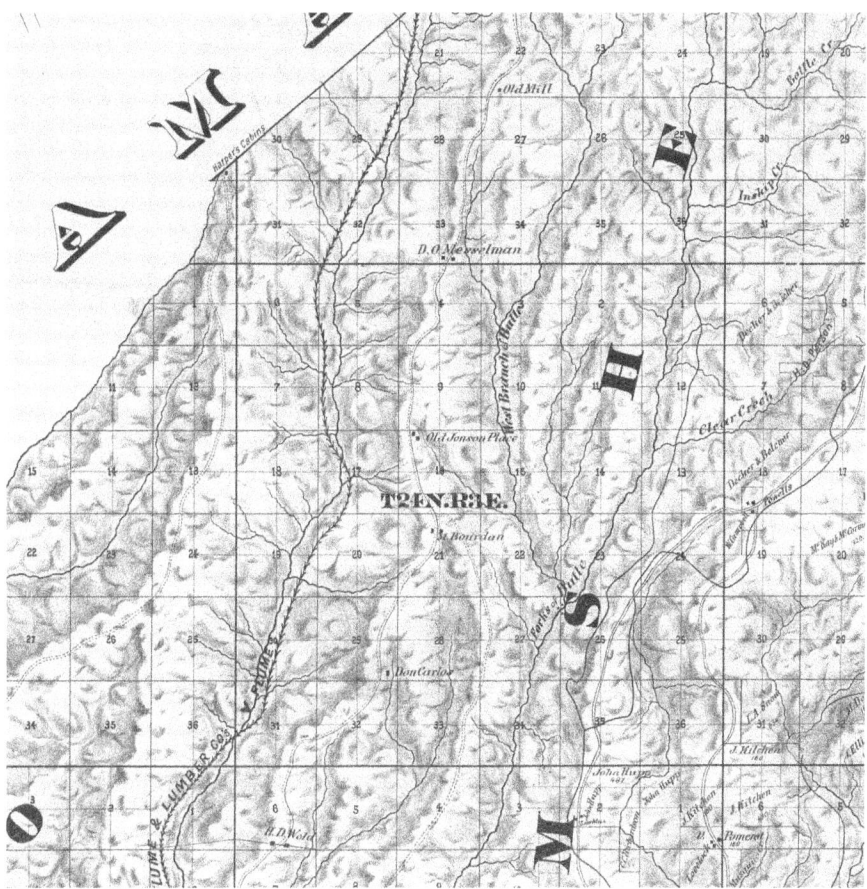

Middle third of the Butte County portion of Chico and Humboldt Wagon Road, showing Musselman's (spelled incorrectly on map), located about nine miles up the road from Weld's. From *Official Map of the County of Butte, California, 1877*, compiled by James McGann. *Courtesy of Library of Congress.*

accommodations. Under their watch, the place became known as Forest Ranch. Barnard and Wm. Bonham eventually purchased Finley's sawmill,[90] possibly around the time the Welds bought Findley's house.

Myron Berdan obtained the place formerly known as the Hornback stand, about four miles farther up the road, and the popular stopping point fittingly became known as Berdan's. The cold water at this place came from a well eighty feet deep and was drawn up by horse power.[91]

About twenty-five miles from Chico, Uncle Jo Campbell built a ballroom on his place, called Campbell's station, and had weekly dances that covered two nights in succession.[92] There was also a sawmill located there.[93] D.O.

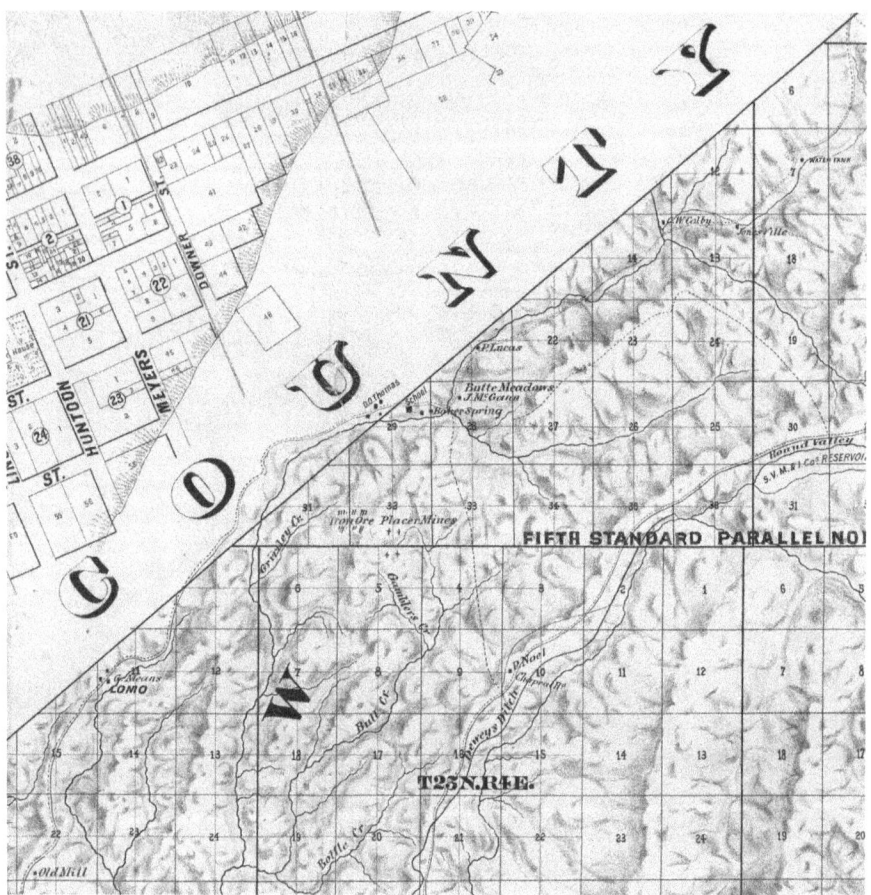

Upper third of Butte County portion of Chico and Humboldt Wagon Road. Shortly after Lomo, the road passed through Tehama County for a few miles before returning to Butte County near Butte Meadows. In the upper right corner of the map, it entered Plumas County near the Tehama County line. From *Official Map of the County of Butte, California, 1877*, compiled by James McGann. *Courtesy of Library of Congress.*

Musselman purchased Campbell's station in 1873 and opened the Mountain House, advertising that he could accommodate guests with comfortable rooms, a bar and a billiard table.[94] Around this time, Bonham and Aldersley had a lumber mill called the Yelper operating here.[95] George W. Bennett took over the way station sometime later,[96] and the place was soon referred to as the West Branch.

Mr. Sewell acquired the Hog's Back property sometime in the early 1870s, and the place was eventually referred to as Lomo.[97] In the middle of the decade, Mr. and Mrs. Means took over the establishment. The couple kept up the Lomo House for travelers and maintained a fine orchard.[98] Located three-quarters of a mile from the Victor Mill, a good number of families settled in Lomo, and Mr. Means provided a schoolhouse and teacher for the children, at his own expense. Early on, he felt justified asking for assistance from the Chico School District but was having no luck. A year later, he was hoping the board of supervisors would create a new district instead of having his patrons carry the burden.[99]

Although it's uncertain exactly when it happened, the Sutton House was built and operated by John Sutton for a while. Located in the scenic Butte Meadows area, it became part of Tehama County after the county line was resurveyed in 1874. Early in the decade, the place didn't see much action, but it eventually became a popular stopping place on the road. In the summer of 1873, it was reported that the little community had a school with eleven pupils. In hopes of increasing the student body, a couple of summer homes were made available rent-free on the condition that the occupants furnish one or two pupils for the school.[100] By 1876, the learning facility, with about twenty children in attendance, received help from Tehama and Butte Counties. In March 1875, the Sutton House, then belonging to D.O. Thomas, burned down. The cause was a defective stove pipe.[101] When it reopened in June the same year, it was initiated by a grand ball.[102] Afterward, it became a resort bustling with life, offering various outdoor activities—such as hunting and fishing—and featuring dancing and a fine croquet court. Late in the decade, the Sutton House burned down again (this time arson was suspected) when Mr. Carter owned the establishment, but Watson C. Roberts was leasing and managing it at the time.[103] And like a phoenix rising from the ashes, the house was rebuilt once more, and even better.[104] Nearby were a couple of dairy and stock ranches—the Lucas place and McGann's ranch, the latter of which was well known for its potatoes and timothy hay. The Lucas place was a summer range for the cattle that the family raised on the ranch in Big Chico Creek Canyon.

A little less than two miles west of Sutton House was the Arcade Springs, located near the Arcade Mill. In 1875, Dr. William King, the proprietor of the springs, which were originally discovered by Colonel Baker, turned the place into a popular resort. He built a hotel, erected several cottages and provided a bathhouse, while touting the mineral waters—containing sulfur, iron, soda and more—that were said to have curative properties that could overcome many diseases.[105] One ad in particular claimed the mountain climate was beneficial to those suffering from consumption and related diseases, while the water treatment and climate, in combination, could swiftly lead to a permanent cure for rheumatism, diseases of the kidney, dyspepsia, female complaints and other afflictions.[106]

A little over half a mile up the road from the Sutton House was the Baker Spring, which was also discovered by Colonel Baker. It, too, boasted water with restorative ingredients, and invalids were invited to give it a try.[107]

In 1870, Colonel Baker handed out sets of bells as prizes for best teams on the Chico and Humboldt Wagon Road. Three men won the gift, the top one hauling 7,722 feet of lumber with eight mules.[108] Bells were often used on lead horses as warnings to teamsters approaching curves from the opposite direction on narrow roads, such as Bidwell's road.

Jonesville, the last resort area before climbing up the steep grade to the Big Summit, continued to be popular with people from Chico as a summer place to relax and escape the heat of the valley. A correspondent to the *Northern Enterprise* even suggested that the refreshing mountain environment surrounding the school up there was invigorating to students and promoted the search for knowledge, as opposed to the apathy and indifference seen in the valley.[109] She may have had a point. There was no mechanical air conditioning in those days, and it must have been hard to concentrate during days of stifling heat in the low country. The mountain communities,

Bells were used on horses to warn approaching vehicles around sharp corners. *Courtesy of CSU, Chico, Meriam Library, Special Collections.*

1870s: A Postal Route Established

Team of horses on Chico and Humboldt Wagon Road with bells on. *Courtesy of CSU, Chico, Meriam Library, Special Collections.*

on the other hand, had the benefit of natural air conditioning with those cool breezes passing through regularly. Another ranch in the area, owned by G.W. Colby, was located just down the road from Jonesville.

The news reported that Job Dye lived in the place situated in the mountain meadows a few miles east of the Big Summit.[110] Later, Mike Bruce resided here.[111]

Some statistics about travel on the road during 1877 were published the following year in a local paper. Mr. J.E. Carter, the superintendent of the road, reported that 3,720 horse teams, ranging from 1 to 12 horses each, passed by tollgate no. 1 at the Fourteen-Mile House. Horsemen, packs and led horses, loose stock and sheep amounted to another 5,928 passing through this same pay station. It was also reported that 1,086 horse teams, ranging from 1 to 10 horses each, passed through tollgate no. 2, located at Mike Bruce's place, about forty-eight miles from Chico. Sheep, loose stock cattle, loose horses, saddle horses and pack and led horses amounted to another 27,111 animals, with the sheep making up 84 percent of that amount. The toll collected that year was $6,493.36. Daily stage travel was implemented in the spring and lasted through the summer. By winter, it was reduced to semi-weekly.[112]

With that amount of traffic, it was evident that the road was being used quite a bit and seemed to justify the establishment of a postal route with offices between Chico and Prattville. The citizens living along the Chico and Humboldt Wagon Road certainly felt so and had been pleading for one since the early part of the decade.[113] However, getting the process underway was slow. By the latter part of the decade, it was estimated that between 750 and 1,000 settlers, miners and mill hands made the mountains their home for six months out of the year, and the paper argued that they should have mail facilities.[114] Until then, anyone who wanted mail matter had to have it sent by expensive express. Finally, in 1878, post offices along the road were established at Forest Ranch, Berdan's, West Branch, Lomo and Butte Meadows.

The winter of 1873–74 was a rough one for residents on the higher part of the road, particularly the Jonesville area, where homes and barns crumbled under the weight of the deep snow. Susanville was hit hard too. A letter from that town, written from John Anthony to Sandy Young, informed the Chico butcher that the stock in the area was decimated by the harsh winter, and some ranchers lost anywhere from one-half to all of their herd.[115]

The 1875–76 winter was bad as well, and the area around Butte Meadows again took a big hit. In February, nine feet of snow had piled up on the ground around the Sutton House, crushing more buildings.[116] In April of that same year, it was reported that the bridge over Butte Creek beyond Thomas's was washed away, and the money to build a new one was nowhere in sight.[117] Fortunately, something was done about that because it was repaired by late May.[118]

Like the road, the logging industry in the area went through some big transformations. The most noteworthy was due to C.F. Ellsworth's dissatisfaction with the cost of hauling his forest product. Like any lumberman of that era, Ellsworth soon realized that hauling rough lumber from the mills in the higher elevations to the finishing plants below was expensive. So, hearing of the successful application of V-flumes to transport lumber, he investigated the possibility of such an operation in Big Chico Creek or Butte Creek Canyons to get his lumber down from the foothills and mountains. However, a prominent local surveyor informed him that it couldn't be done, and that likely prompted Ellsworth to sell his lumber properties to W.K. Springer sometime in late 1870 or early 1871[119] and move his operations to Tehama County, where the terrain appeared to better accommodate fluming.

Ellsworth soon began fulfilling his vision, and before it was even finished, others could see its potential. A trend was in the making. Ellsworth's success inspired another look at Big Chico Creek,[120] and Colonel H.B. Shackelford, Tehama County surveyor, declared that building a flume along Big Chico Creek was feasible after all. In November 1872, it was reported that a new joint stock company was formed to do just that,[121] and on May 2, 1873, the Butte Flume and Lumber Company filed a certificate of incorporation with the secretary of state. The trustees of the new company were three Woodsum brothers (O.P., A.C. and V.B.) and the previously established partnership of B.F. Allen, G.M. Taylor and C.H. Holbrook.[122] When the flume made its first big run of lumber in September 1874,[123] three mills, all located at the upper end of Big Chico Creek, were feeding it lumber. The Cascade and Belmont mills were owned by the Butte Flume and Lumber Company. The Arcade Mill, located near the soon-to-be Dr. King mineral spring resort, belonged to the McCormick brothers.[124] The Arcade Mill burned in 1877, when the McCormick brothers no longer owned it. The machinery was saved, and it was quickly rebuilt.[125]

The Big Chico Creek flume traveled a distance of thirty-three miles to its original end point, later referred to as the Old Dump, where Jason Springer's sash and door plant and a planing mill were established. At first, the flume didn't go all the way to the town of Chico because farmers along the last piece of right-of-way were asking too much for permission to go through their land.[126] However, in 1876, John Bidwell purchased the necessary land to allow the lumber firm to extend the flume another three and a half miles to the final terminating point at East Eighth and Pine Streets in Chico.[127] When it did so, the old lumber unloading station was bypassed. The Old Dump and the surrounding community survived for a time afterward by receiving lumber on wagons from some foothill mills unconnected to the flume, including the aforementioned Victor Mill near Lomo, which was owned by Jason Springer and Co.[128] Unfortunately, in April 1878, the sash factory at the Old Dump burned to the ground. With no insurance, Springer and Co. had no plans to rebuild it, threatening the very survival of the little town.[129]

Before the flume was extended, however, the Butte Flume and Lumber Company was taken over by the Sierra Flume and Lumber Company. Incorporated in November 1875,[130] the new company swallowed up land and many other lumber interests in northeastern California, including the Arcade Mill, making it a giant in the industry. The Chico division, one of three, included the Big Chico Creek flume and associated mills and yards. In 1876, it was reported that the daily cutting capacity of the Cascade Mill was thirty-five thousand feet, the Belmont twenty thousand feet and the Arcade

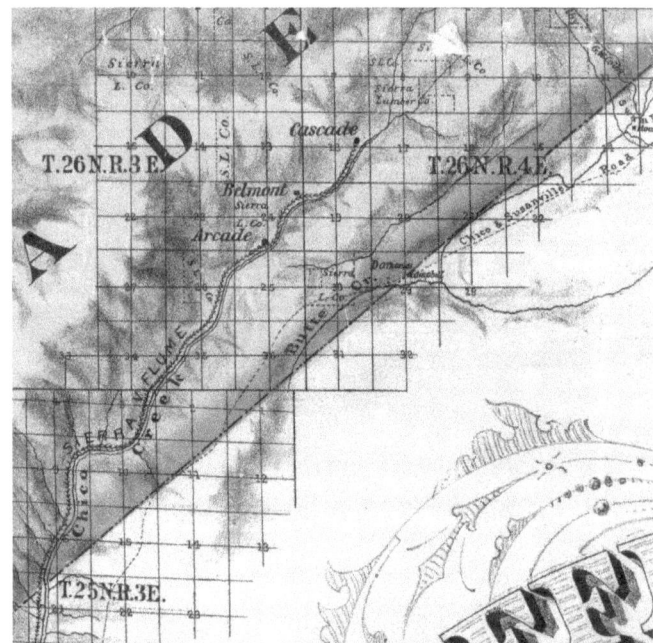

Location of the three mills at the head of the Big Chico Creek V-flume. From *Official Map of the County of Tehama, California, 1878*, compiled by H.B. Shackelford and F.J. Nugent. *Courtesy of Library of Congress.*

Logs being loaded onto a "truck" to be transported to the mill on a tramway. Sketch drawn by Will L. Taylor, circa 1877. *Courtesy of CSU, Chico, Meriam Library, Special Collections.*

twenty-one thousand feet. The Cascade had thirty-nine workers and the Belmont and Arcade each had thirty. Twenty-four more were required to operate the flume, which could transport seventy thousand feet of lumber a day.[131] In 1877, it was reported that Chico's sash and door factory was running with a daily capacity of two hundred doors, one hundred windows and fifty blinds. The planing mill there specialized in flooring, ceiling, wainscoting, stepping, shingles, laths, pickets, mouldings, brackets, door and window frames and more.[132]

It wasn't long before there were concerns that the Sierra Flume and Lumber Company monopoly was going to be bad for the community by squeezing out the little guys and naming its own price for lumber.[133] This, and its practice of hiring a good number of Chinese people at the expense of whites,[134] made the company unpopular with a large segment of the locals. So, when the company suspended operations in July 1878, which led to bankruptcy,[135] there were not a lot of tears.[136] Although the financial panic in San Francisco and the California drought didn't help the situation, it was clear that the company's short existence was mostly a result of overproduction and going into severe debt. As one newspaper put it, "The Sierra Flume & Lumber Company was managed too much in the old army style, with too much red tape and little practical business ability, hence its failure."[137]

Later that year, the Sierra Lumber Company was incorporated to take over the Sierra Flume and Lumber interests. Although initially under the control of some of the same individuals who put the previous company in ruin, an improving economic environment and better management practices made this newest version of big lumber a successful enterprise for almost thirty years until the Diamond Match Company bought out the last of its properties in 1907.

The wooden V-flume was shaped like the name implies. It was generally four feet across at top water level, had thirty-two-inch sloping sides and was about sixteen inches wide at the bottom. It was made in sixteen-foot sections referred to as boxes. Starting from the Cascade Mill, the flume slithered along the curves of Big Chico Creek Canyon like a giant serpent. The height of the flume varied in accordance with the terrain. Sometimes it would lay on cribbing close to the ground. Other times it would rest high up on trestlework as much as one hundred feet in the air. Walkways were built alongside the waterway for access to make repairs or help move the lumber along. The builders tried to keep a constant grade, but the rugged terrain would not allow it, so much of the time, the waters moved gently along at about ten miles per hour, but there were also stretches that it might average thirty miles per hour or more.

Despite the big savings in transportation costs it provided, the expense of building the Big Chico Creek flume was huge. The original thirty-three miles cost more than $150,000.[138]

Maintaining the flume was not cheap either, especially when long sections would come down and need to be replaced. Although severe storms would often take out the flume in many places,[139] the area around the Old Dump seemed to be particularly vulnerable. In January 1875, high winds knocked down about eighty or ninety feet of trestlework above the Old Dump,[140] and in May 1878, these same forces blew down about twenty-five boxes of the tall trestlework in the same general vicinity.[141] In January 1878, about three-quarters of a mile was blown down between the Old and New Dumps.[142]

One might wonder if the Big Chico Creek V-flume was good for trout fishing. Well, not generally; however, on at least one occasion the aquatic creatures managed to find a way in, and the boys at the dump took advantage of the situation in a way that almost didn't seem fair. As the wayward swimmers tried to get by the waiting workers, they were easy prey. A simple thump on the head with a club, and dinner plans were set.[143]

Speaking of trout, shortly after Sierra Lumber took over, there were complaints about the mills at the headwaters of Big Chico Creek dumping large amounts of sawdust into the stream. (This was a disposal practice sometimes used by lumber mills that would periodically get exposed.) The editor of the *Chico Enterprise* couldn't understand why the mills didn't willingly burn the sawdust or at least move it farther from the water so that the spawning grounds would not be destroyed. If nothing else, the paper suggested a heavy fine might provide the incentive.[144]

Returning to the flume, people would make vehicles to transport themselves down the waterway. These means of conveyance came in various shapes and sizes. Sometimes passengers would sit on top of a flat surface made of boards fastened together. Other times, they might sit inside a watercraft that had sides that were designed to fit in the sloping walls of the flume. Either way, it could be a risky venture. Passengers had to be constantly on the alert for overhanging rocks, downed branches or trees, lumber jams or even breaks in the structure. The walkways would often be slippery from water or ice. Therefore, the company forbade the public from riding on the flume, and employees were allowed to do it only when it was necessary.[145]

Along the length of the flume, stations were located at strategic points that housed flume tenders (also known as lumber herders), who were company

1870s: A Postal Route Established

Parallel flumes indicated that there was a "switch" nearby for diverting water flow. *Courtesy of CSU, Chico, Meriam Library, Special Collections.*

This double-hooked pick-a-roon was used by lumber herders on Sierra Lumber's Empire lumber flume, so it was likely used by workers along Big Chico Creek too. *Courtesy of CSU, Chico, Meriam Library, Special Collections.*

employees who maintained the flume and kept things in running order. These watchmen tried to discourage the public from riding the flume or walking on the sidewalk. However, the danger that it posed could not deter people from the convenience or the thrills the waterway offered.

Flume tenders herded the lumber with a tool referred to as a pick-a-roon. Used for moving logs and lumber, pick-a-roons came in many shapes and sizes. One thing they all had in common was a sharp point at the head that was used to stick into the wood and maneuver it around.

Flirting in the Mountains

Recall that the town of Jonesville was located about six or seven miles up the road from the Empire Mill in Butte Meadows. Early in the decade, the Butte Meadows and Jonesville region hadn't yet developed into the bustling resort area it would soon become. The following story begins when a correspondent from the Empire Mill wrote to a valley paper and noted that the people of Chico and the vicinity appeared to be streaming up to the mountains in droves to escape the heat and dust of the lowlands and indulge in the healthy atmosphere of higher elevations. With this sudden influx of valley folk, it seems the mountain mill boys eagerly anticipated socializing with some members of the not-so-commonly-seen opposite sex.

However, there were issues, as the writer explained in the July 30, 1870 *Northern Enterprise*:

> *Jonesville—a few weeks since but an echo of Goldsmith's Deserted Village, has assumed the proportion and aspect of a fashionable watering place, and almost every day brings along beveys* [sic] *of fair girls, all destined to this earthly Heaven. This may be for a while; but we never knew it otherwise than that the boys will follow, and these nuns of the mountain convent, in all their shyness, will be peeking from behind every rock and shrub to get a glimpse at some favored beaux of other days. The Empire has also her share of guests this season, which adds much to our life and enjoyment. We have had several parties here lately, which passed off very pleasantly. They were, however, surprise. We had so long been accustomed to all work and no play, that we had almost forgotten how to enjoy pleasure, but when once we got on our "store clothes," and our faces washed, we could work ourselves up into an enthusiasm which reminded us of the days when we were young. If you*

have anybody else left, send them up; we like to see them. Their sociability and good appearance will be a passport to good society anywhere.

Shortly after, a young lady presented a spirited rebuttal to the same newspaper, with a challenge for the previous writer. The August 13, 1870 *Northern Enterprise* printed her response:

We have seen, by the last Enterprise, the effusion of a correspondent from the Empire Mills, who, in speaking of the Jonesville ladies, calls them convent nuns, who peke [sic] from behind rock, bush and tree, to obtain sight of their lovers who come to visit them. Please inform him that though styled "tender-hearted maidens," we are not the cowards he would publish us, but that we have that conscious rectitude, and moral bravery, which enables us to meet those we love face to face, and hand in hand. Rather think your correspondent was laboring under some strange hallucination which caused him to forget the place and the sex of his subject. It is a well-known custom of the "mills," that when ladies pass, all hands, forgetting their employment, are posted behind rocks, trees and shop cracks, looking as if they had never seen a woman before, as if afraid an open sight would frighten them. Bid your correspondent, Mr. Editor, come and see us, and we will show him that no such custom prevails here.

THE CONDITION OF THE ROAD

As to be expected after years of heavy use, the road would often become very rough in spots, making it the subject of much criticism. A lot of the unevenness could be attributed to the many teams with lumber that constantly passed over it.[146] The portion that traversed the bare Tuscan Formation was especially troublesome, as reported in the August 2, 1872 *Northern Enterprise*:

A GROWL AT THE ROAD. —A correspondent who has been over a portion of the Humboldt road complains bitterly of its roughness, and says it is an imposition to charge toll for riding over the first sixteen miles from Chico. He suggests to the lessees the filling up of the chuck holes with bark or other substance that will hold together, and not loose dirt that is carried off by every puff of wind. If they won't do it, he will bring the subject before the Chico Young Men's Christian Association, and have them look after the

Worn-down ruts can still be seen today as the old road begins to ascend the foothills through the hard and rocky Tuscan Formation. *Photo by author.*

matter, as a means of stopping the profanity of the teamsters, who cannot help cursing the road and those who own it. Our correspondent is astonished that a livery stable lets out a vehicle to go over this road, as his buggy was nearly shivered to pieces by the jolting over the rocks.

Displeasure with the highway often began right out of the gate, as expressed by this reporter in a September 17, 1875 *Chico Enterprise* article: "Leaving Chico on the stage at the early hour of four o'clock A.M., we crossed the limits of the Town Incorporation and entered the Humboldt avenue, and such an avenue—one mile and a half of ruts, holes a foot deep, and not less than twenty inches of dust on the level...."

Sometimes Mother Nature had the final say, and circumstances were simply not under the control of man. Heavy snowfall was one of these situations, and it occasionally got deep on the Big Summit. For instance, it was reported in March 1874 that eighteen to twenty feet had accumulated on the highest point of the Chico and Humboldt Wagon Road.[147] These conditions likely closed the highway for some time. However, this did not mean it was always impassable after heavy snows. It just meant that the travelers had to adapt. Recall that horses with sleighs were sometimes used over the summit, but at times other preparations had to be made too. For instance, when the crust became very hard, blankets were wrapped around the legs of horses to prevent them from getting lacerated.[148]

LIVESTOCK CELEBRATE NEW YEAR EARLY

William "Billy" Boness (sometimes spelled Bonness in the news) lived near Little Chico Creek east of the Ten-Mile House. William was known as an expert hunter, and for many years, the local newspapers would occasionally write stories about his noted prowess in bringing down mountain lions and bears. For instance, in 1875, it was reported that he killed four lions in one week—a large haul by anyone's standards. The local residents, whose livestock were being depredated by the large felines, must have appreciated his efforts immensely.[149] However, keeping his personal livestock under control was a different story, as the December 6, 1872 *Northern Enterprise* explained:

> *Wm. Bonness, of Little Chico Creek, left home one day this week with his family to spend the day with a neighbor. In his yard were two casks of wine and some cattle, horses and hogs. In the evening, when he returned, he found all his domestic animals on a spree. They had upset the casks of wine and from the pools upon the ground slaked their thirst. The consequence was a general drunk, and when he observed horses reeling,*

cattle staggering and pigs dead or squealing, he fancied the horse disease had broken out, and at once commenced to administer bacon and grease. He says the true disposition of the drunkard was shown in the hogs.

BIZARRE MURDER ON THE ROAD

Milton Cain was no stranger to controversy or being in the news. During 1859, he was a central figure in a confrontation between Butte Creek miners and a group of valley men who, under the authority of state officials, were sent to round up Indians working with miners for removal to reservations. At the time, Cain was one of several gold seekers in the area known to be cohabitating with an Indian woman, an act considered highly immoral by many of the valley people. While living in Butte Creek, Cain was reported to have killed an Indian for coming around his premises.[150]

Fast-forward to 1875. Milton Cain now lived about twenty miles from Chico on the Chico and Humboldt Wagon Road, at the site of the old Comet Mill, which ceased operating about four years earlier. Some of the buildings were left standing, and Cain lived in one of them. It was reported that he once shared it for a while with a woman by the name of Susan Rank, otherwise known as Mrs. Franklin or Widow Franklin. (Franklin later denied she ever lived in the same house as Cain.)

Mrs. Franklin was known for threatening the lives of several people[151] and was no stranger to the news. The previous year, a local paper printed a story about how she had been found lying drunk in the snow on the Chico and Humboldt Wagon Road by a man traveling on snowshoes. The man couldn't get the inebriated woman out of her stupor enough to move her to a protected place. So, after the passerby reported the incident at Lee's place, the nearest station along the road, a company of men went out to look for her.[152] Franklin obviously survived the incident because, as we shall see, she wasn't done supplying local papers with some interesting material.

Charles Davies, "Don Carlos," lived in the area. Around February 1875, Cain and Franklin allegedly tried to claim jump his land by burning down his cabin in his absence. Before they did, though, they took his blankets. When Charles tried to lay claim to the covers, Franklin went after him with a pistol. Cain eventually returned the blankets.

By now, the reader should have realized that these two people were trouble with a capital *T*. In March 1875, the terror resurfaced in a big way.

1870s: A Postal Route Established

James Dorland had bought the old Comet Mill site and buildings from W.K. Springer the previous summer and was making preparations with his son, George, to take over and develop it for his wants.[153] The problem was that during the previous fall, Cain had been doing some work on the same land, which he thought was abandoned, and filed a claim on it. A dispute was in the making.

Cain told Dorland that if he could show proof of ownership, he would drop his claim and leave. In the meantime, the following sign (which was written by Franklin since Cain couldn't read or write) was posted on a tree near a spring, according to Charles Davies's testimony at the coroner's inquest, as reported in the April 3, 1875 *Weekly Butte Record*: "Notice—All persons are forbidden tearing down fence or interfering with this spring. I will protect my home with my life. Signed, Milton Cain."

Then things got really ugly. This is how it went down, according to George Dorland's testimony at the same inquest, as reported in the April 3, 1875 *Weekly Butte Record*:

> *Father and I were down at the old Comet Mill. We knocked off some boards to make a door for the house in which we were living. After getting the boards we started up hill towards the house with them. Father was carrying one board, and I the other. I was about fifteen or twenty yards ahead. Heard report of a gun, and father exclaim, "Oh dear," "Oh dear,". Should judge from the report that it was a rifle. Turned around upon hearing the report and exclamation, and saw father falling, as he fell he exclaimed again in a faint voice "Oh dear," at the same time saw a man with gun in right hand running under the slabway of the mill. Had known him but a few days, but recognized him as a man by the name of Cain.*

According to his testimony, George then ran from the scene to get his gun and was eventually joined by neighbors Myron Berdan and Charles Davies. The three of them went back to where the body lay. After inspecting fresh tracks in the snow and mud from the man who appeared to be the shooter, Berdan determined they were probably made by Cain.

Milton Cain immediately went on the lam. Sheriff Daniels figured he was probably still in the area, so the lawman formed a posse with six other men, who were soon in hot pursuit. The problem was that in these foothill canyons there were many places a fugitive could conceal himself while friends helped him. So, taking no chances, the sheriff went from one cabin to the next, and after interrogating the inhabitants, he made each of them join the party so that he could keep an eye on them. Cain was eventually caught and placed under custody, thanks to the strategy of Sheriff Daniels.[154] As the April 9, 1875 *Northern Enterprise* reported:

> *In this connection to [sic] much credit cannot be accorded to Sheriff Daniels for the manner in which he has acted throughout in this affair, and the keen detective qualities shown in his management of the hunt and the arrest. Had he allowed any of the parties to separate on Monday night, Cain would have still been at large, and there is no telling where he could have been found, as the hiding places in these canyons are known only to a few old pioneers, and a secret sympathy and telegraphy exists among them which is calculated to evade all pursuit.*

As indicated, this code of solidarity among established locals apparently extended beyond the boundaries of the law. Cain had been in the area for more than fifteen years, while James Dorland was a relative newcomer who had been in Butte County for about three years and on the ridge even shorter.

The thrill of the pursuit turned out to be a little more than one of the posse members had bargained for. J.C. Morgan had "given out" early on the second day of the chase and was instructed to go back to camp and wait for the others to arrive. The problem was that Morgan got lost and proceeded to fight through the thick chaparral that covered the steep canyon walls. When the disoriented man managed to crawl down to the bottom of the canyon, he felt compelled to cross icy cold Butte Creek with the water practically up to his head. The exhausted posse member eventually made it to the community of Nimshew on the other side of the creek and then the rest of the way into Chico, while a search party was hopelessly trying to find him.

You might think that was the end of the story. Not so fast! Widow Franklin was still on the loose. About six months after the murder, Cain's former girlfriend met with a man known as Phillips, the person she suspected of turning in the killer. After engaging in a conversation with Phillips and waiting for the right moment, Franklin pulled Phillips's hunting knife from its sheath and proceeded to slice his throat with it. Although the cut was a nasty one, Phillips was expected to survive. Franklin was in the news once more.[155]

1870s: A Postal Route Established

A Curious Case, Indeed

In 1876, a man by the name of Tubbs arrived in Chico, missing his hat, coat and blankets and with a bullet wound in his left arm and a slight injury to his shoulder. After receiving medical attention, he gave an account to the townspeople of what the newspaper referred to as a "curious case." Tubbs explained that he was traveling up the Chico and Humboldt Wagon Road on foot when he decided to take a rest about a mile above Musselman's (incorrectly spelled "Mussleman" in the following news story). While Tubbs was resting and looking at some paper, a man with a mule came along, dismounted and stuck a gun in his face, telling him to throw up his hands.

At about this time, the mule became frightened at something and ran off from the man, who was holding it by a rope. Tubbs seized the opportunity and grasped the barrel of the revolver, but his attacker still had the handle. While struggling with the man, Tubbs assumed he was being robbed and offered to give the guy whatever money he had, but the assailant told him he was going to kill him for murdering his brother. As the struggle continued, the man claimed to be an officer of the law wanting to arrest Tubbs. Although he didn't believe him, Tubbs said he finally grew so exhausted from the long struggle that he agreed to go with the man. A reporter for the June 17, 1876 *Weekly Butte Record* continued with the rest of Tubbs's wild story:

> His assailant then proposed to tie him. Tubbs says it occurred to him that if he submitted to this, he would be shot and thrown in the canyon, and when his assailant stooped to pick up a piece of rope to tie him, he made a break and ran for life. It was then he received his wounds. He kept on, however, taking the back track to Mussleman's. His assailant's mule ran on ahead of him. Arriving at Mussleman's he told the people there he had been shot, and desired to be taken to Chico. Mr. Mussleman told him he had no team, or horses and could not. He then told Mr. Mussleman that the mule belonged to the man who had shot him, and desired to have him caught so he could ride him to Chico. This was declined, and Tubbs, thinking that all were in partnership with his assailant, lit out for Chico on foot, as rapidly as his condition would permit. After climbing the hill, this side of Mussleman's, to avoid any pursuit, he traveled outside of the road. Arriving in Chico, he told his story and exhibited his wounds to the astonishment of nearly the entire population, who kept up a running comment upon the probabilities of the case. Constable Hegan was dispatched up the Humboldt road to arrest the man, and he was lodged

Mountain House

THIS old and popular Mountain stand is situated on the Humboldt Road, distant twenty-five miles from Chico.

Having purchased the interest of Jo. Campbell to the premises, I have remodeled and refurnished the House, and can now offer the public the best of accommodation.

**Comfortable Rooms,
Good Beds,
The Best of Fare.**

My Bar is supplied with the best Brands of **Wines and Liquors**, and a

First-Class Billiard Table.

Every attention paid my customers.
ap3-1mo   D. O. MUSSELMAN.

This April 24, 1874 *Chico Enterprise* ad spelled Musselman's name correctly.

in jail on Sunday. His name is Sanders, and he was formerly a resident of Dayton. His story is to the effect that he undertook to arrest Tubbs for killing his cattle, and says that when told that was why he was arresting him, Tubbs replied that he did not kill his brother, and had never killed anybody. Says his pistol went off accidently when Tubbs was wounded. That he used to consider himself a good foot racer, but that in running some 60 yards after Tubbs, he thinks the latter beat him at least 70 yards, and must have beaten the mule into Mussleman's.

Sanders was charged with assault to commit murder and was soon out on bail. The outcome of his trial is unknown. Proceedings against Tubbs for killing the cattle owned by Sanders were dropped because he proved to have an alibi. This seems like one of those stories in which it is difficult to determine who to believe—Tubbs, Sanders or even the reporter.

The Soap Man Gets Robbed on the Big Summit

One didn't have to be on a stage to get robbed on the Chico and Humboldt Wagon Road. Anyone was fair game. Take Mr. Twitchell, for example, who was heading to Plumas County to deliver a load of soap one day. While stopped on the Big Summit to work on his brakes before descending the steep slope, Twitchell unexpectedly felt the weight of a heavy hand on his shoulder.

The August 10, 1877 *Chico Enterprise* reported:

> *Not supposing that any one was near him, his first thoughts were that he was in the paws of some huge grizzly which had crept stealthily upon him. He shook and trembled worse than ever he did with the ague, and he has had his share of that, but the words, in a broken accent, "What have you got in your wagon?" recalled him to his senses. "Soap," was the involuntary reply. "Soap be——, how much money have you got?" A new light dawned upon Twitchell, he was in the hands of robbers. Another sprang up behind him and seized both his arms and crossed them at his back, bending him backwards, while the other went through his pockets, searched the box in the wagon, and all they got for their pains was a quarter of a dollar and a plug of tobacco. They chided him for shaking so, and threatened to kill him if he had not more money the next time they met. There were four of them in sight and one in the brush, who, he thinks was an American, the other four being Spaniards, and thought to belong to the band of vaqueros, some twenty in number, who are in the employ of John Boggs, in the vicinity of Deer Creek Meadows. Twitchell started out this week again with a load, and if he meets them will give them a warm reception.*

Accidents Along the Road and at the Mills

The Chico and Humboldt Wagon Road could be dangerous for man and beast. Noteworthy accidents, with some fatalities, were occasionally reported in the news.

Sometimes the grade posed a problem, like when a jolt during a speedy descent knocked Francis Rogers off his seat and threw him under the wheels of the wagon he was riding in, injuring him considerably.[156] One didn't have to be going downhill to get injured either. While ascending a steep grade called Dead Man's Hill, a man named Montgomery was walking alongside his wagon when he somehow got tangled in a wheel and was dragged along before the wheel passed over him, causing severe leg injuries.[157]

Equines caused injuries too. James McVey was hauling water in a cart to the Ten-Mile House one day when he was kicked in the face by one of these unruly beasts and was knocked senseless into the brush,[158] prompting the editor of the *Enterprise* to later remark, "The wound is healing fast, but Jim will bear the marks of that mule's foot in his face as long as he lives."[159]

Just a few months later, Elias Findley was kicked in the abdomen by a mule somewhere below the tollhouse while hauling a load of lumber. At first, Findley thought he could continue to his destination and even stopped along the way at James McVey's for dinner. Eventually, however, the pain became so excruciating that he was compelled to leave his team and attempt to walk for help. The injured teamster finally realized he could go no farther and was found lying in the road by a passerby who assisted him to the next stop, Hog Springs, where a messenger was sent to Chico for medical assistance.[160] Those two incidents were painful, but at least McVey and Findley survived. The same couldn't be said for Sol. Bartol, who was killed when he was thrown from his horse and fell under a wagon.[161]

Equines themselves weren't immune to accidents and injuries either. Going down a grade about twenty miles from Chico, the brakes failed on a loaded wagon driven by one of W.K. Springer's teamsters, causing it to shoot forward and run over a horse and mule, killing the unfortunate animals.[162] A teamster named Schimler, who worked for D.M. Reavis, once allowed his six mules to get off the grade near the Ten-Mile House, causing the team and wagon to fall down the embankment about thirty feet. It was amazing that no one was injured, and the damage to the rig was minimal.[163]

Maybe the most spectacular incident of the 1870s, though, was carried out by F.G. Hail and his wife, who were going down the north side of the Big Summit with horses and a wagon. The June 15, 1878 *Plumas National*, a Quincy paper, reported the near disaster:

> *While Mr. F.G. Hail and his bride were returning from Chico, last week and when just this side of the summit, they met with quite an accident, but fortunately escaped without injury. While coming down a hill, the hinder part of the wagon tipped forward, turning a somersalt [sic] and lighting upon the horses. Mr. and Mrs. Hail jumped out in time to avoid the catastrophe, and the team, after running a short distance, were captured. The doubletree and harness were somewhat injured but beyond that no serious consequences resulted. We congratulate the young couple on their lucky escape.*

The mountain lumber mills along the road also had their fair share of accidents during this decade. Moving logs were always a danger to workers, resulting in at least three reported fatalities at the Belmont Mill in 1877. Two of them were only one day apart.[164]

As we know, large animals can be unpredictable, and another death occurred when A.M. Spencer was kicked in the chest by an ox while working at the Arcade Mill.[165]

A freak fatality occurred at the Belmont Mill when William Swift simply fell off a wagon backward, about ten feet to the ground, while unloading hay.[166]

Harrowing Escape at the Sutton House

As mentioned earlier, the Sutton House, a popular resort situated among majestic pines, lush green meadows and clear mountain streams on the upper part of the road, burned down for the second time in the decade. The fire began around two o'clock in the morning and spread so quickly that people barely had time to get dressed before they could run for safety.[167] One young lady made the incident a little more frightening than it should have been, as described in the August 2, 1879 *Weekly Butte Record*:

> *From parties present at the burning of the Sutton House we learn of the narrow escape from being burnt to death made by Miss Nettie Elliot. Awakened by the crackling flames and cries of the inmates, she sprang from her bed and rushed out, enveloped in nothing but a* robe de unit. *Collecting herself, she recollected having left her watch, a very valuable one, in the room, and returned to the burning building to get it. She found her room and the watch, and hurrying back, discovered that the staircase, the only method of egress from the burning building, was on fire. To hesitate was certain death, so the young lady bravely plunged into the flame and smoke, and barring a little singeing, came safely down to the foot of the stairs, where her mother stood, crying and wringing her hands at what she thought was her certain destruction.*

Tragedy on the V-Flume

As mentioned, the V-flume was not a safe place to be, especially for people who were not workers for the company and were unfamiliar with the dangers it presented. (Two company employees were reported to have fallen from the flume during this decade—though there were quite possibly more—and both of these men suffered severe bruises.)[168] Although there were many accidents on the Big Chico Creek V-flume during its nearly three and a half decades of operation, the following story describes the only death of a nonemployee that this author is aware of. The story unfolded on a Saturday afternoon when three men went hunting in Big Chico Creek Canyon and decided to return home via the V-flume. The November 17, 1877 *Weekly Butte Record* described the tragic incident as follows:[169]

> *L.L. Cole, Wm. Embry and Erastus McCargar started early in the morning for a hunting trip up Chico Canyon, and after tramping around nearly all day got on one of the lumber jams in the flume thinking to ride down to the Old Dump, where McCargar and Embry lived. They were cautioned about riding on the jam by one of the flume watchmen, and they got off for the time being, but got on again some distance further down. When near the Paul Lucas place another larger jam was discovered in front of them, and McCargar tried to jump off onto the sidewalk, as it is called, but his foot slipped and he fell down from the flume to the ground, a distance of sixty feet. His companions descended to where McCargar*

Flume snaking along high above the ground about four or five miles below the site of McCargar's accident. *Courtesy of CSU, Chico, Meriam Library, Special Collections.*

lay, and found that he was still alive, so they had one of the division men telegraph down to Chico about the accident, and request that help be at once sent out. On learning the news, a messenger from Chico was hastily sent to the Old Dump with the sad news, and from there a wagon was sent to bring the sufferer in. From the time of the accident he lived only a short time, and when the wagon arrived life was extinct.

FOREST DESTRUCTION AND CLIMATE CHANGE

With large-scale logging taking hold in the foothills and lower mountains east of Chico, at least one local paper started expressing concerns about its undesirable consequences, particularly with local climate change. The January 10, 1879 edition of the *Chico Enterprise* reminded its readers of the lessons that Europe and Asia had already learned in regard to the unrestrained destruction of forests, suggesting that it would behoove this nation to take heed. It cited how France, Spain and Italy had seen much of their formerly fertile land turned to barren waste from massive logging practices. It noted how India's policy of cutting without replanting contributed to dangerous periods of alternating flood and drought and resultant famines. It mentioned that Australia was seeing the same effects. It claimed that California and Nevada were experiencing similar climatic changes and that streams that once flowed constantly with natural variations were now showing major ups and downs due to rapid snowmelt from unprotected watersheds.

In the December 6, 1878 edition, the *Chico Enterprise* cited a report made by the secretary of the interior, which accused capitalists and corporations of wanton disregard for the environment and jeopardizing the sustainability of the forests. The paper had this to say:

> *Under the present working of the law our timber lands are fast getting into the hands of lumbers sharps, who care nothing for the requirements of future generations, and only seek to enrich themselves. Our forests are cut clean as they go, and after one section has been denuded and rendered incapable of even growing young trees, the mills are pulled up and moved into another section where the same process is repeated....*
>
> *To the people of California and the Sacramento Valley in particular, this timber question has another and more important interest than the scarcity of fuel and lumber. It is well known that our annual rainfall owes its*

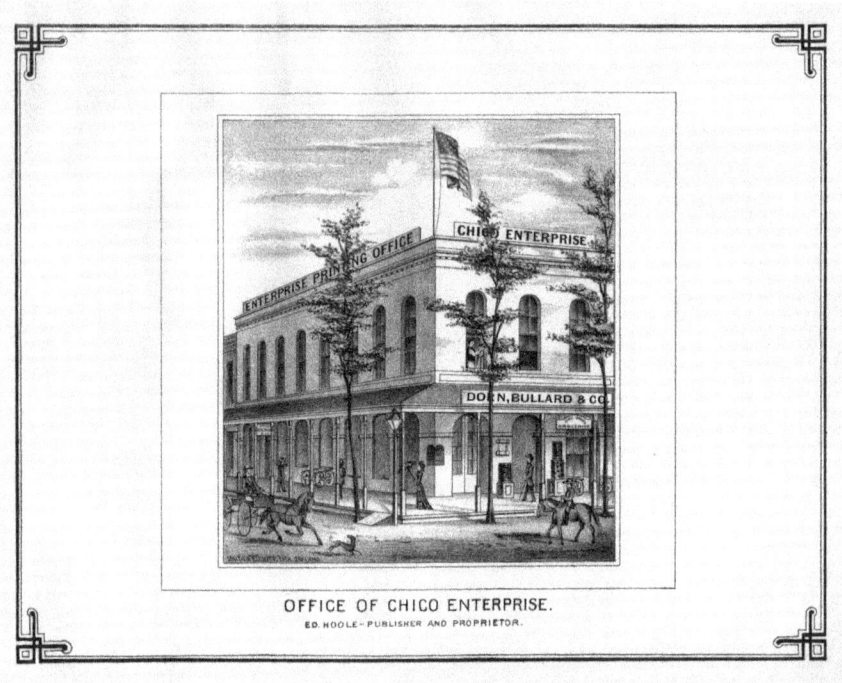

Office of *Chico Enterprise* in the 1870s. *Courtesy of CSU, Chico, Meriam Library, Special Collections.*

regularity and continuance to the forests covering the mountain sides. The clouds in passing over the mountain range precipitate more moisture in a wooded than a barren district. Forests also protect the snow from the direct rays of the sun, and the bulk of it lays in the high altitudes until late in the summer, gradually melting and feeding the streams. It is evident that if this forest protection is removed the snow will melt early in the spring and flood the valley. Then this will be followed by dry, hot weather which will prove death to vegetation, and in time our beautiful valleys will be as barren as portions of Nevada.

Yes, climate change was a concern way back in the 1870s. Of course, it wasn't on the global scale that we hear about today—the overall warming due to excessive emissions from industries and vehicles and from deforestation in tropical rainforests. At this point, they were talking about a much smaller scale. It was about how regional rainfall was being modified. Some might argue that the signs were there—a warning flag had been raised. We knew long ago that humans have the ability to alter the climate.

3
1880s

The Road Charter Expires

OVERVIEW

Although the shacks at Hog Springs were gone by the beginning of this decade, the springs still had plenty of water available.[170] This was a good thing for the thirsty road travelers who were now just six miles out of Chico but had already endured one of the dustiest and roughest parts of the journey.

Early in this decade, the Ten-Mile House was still being kept by Jim McVey, who continued to request compensation for the water that had to be hauled up from the canyon below, unless the user was willing to patronize the bar and table that the establishment also had to offer. In 1881, a Chinese medicine man located at the Ten-Mile House.[171] (Despite a great deal of anti-Chinese sentiment in those days, medicine men appeared to be in high demand, especially after the success of one residing in Deadwood, another part of the county.)

McVey eventually relocated to Forest Ranch and the Brown brothers, Jim and John, moved into the Ten-Mile House.[172] Soon after, the place became known for its organized bear hunts and turkey shoots.[173] The Ten-Mile House burned down in 1886, when James Brown owned it.[174] It was later rebuilt, most likely by Fred Dorrett, who owned the property for a short time afterward, before Brown took over once more.

In April 1880, Paul Lucas, the patriarch of the family, died,[175] leaving his widow, Ellen, with six children to raise. With the help of the older children, the mother continued on with the cattle-raising business.

David Craig was still residing at the Fourteen-Mile House (the old location of the tollgate) for a while, but later in the decade, the Spires family purchased this popular stopping place. There was an orchard, vineyard and garden there. Fred Dorrett leased the hotel and a few acres of land and raised excellent potatoes.[176] Early on in the decade, the new tollgate (one mile farther up the road) inspired some complaints because the tolls were judged as too high—seventy-five cents for a two-horse wagon and other teams charged proportionally.[177]

Horace D. Weld worked hard to develop Forest Ranch into a thriving little community. At the beginning of the decade, it had cottages occupied by families, a hotel for boarders and travelers, a horse-changing station for the Prattville stage and a highly productive garden and orchard.[178] Weld left Forest Ranch by the later part of 1881, and Charles Coppin temporarily took over the postal duties.[179] Not long afterward, Mr. Crabb managed the hotel.[180]

Meanwhile, Wm. Bonham overhauled the Dashaway Mill's old machinery and moved it to a new site about three miles above the old one.[181] (It wasn't long before Bonham was accused of allowing sawdust from this mill to enter Little Chico Creek, killing fish in the waterway.)[182] By the middle of the decade, Captain John Morrison took ownership of the hotel and the Dashaway Mill. Although the hotel was originally managed by Fred Kingsbury,[183] Captain Morrison's wife eventually assumed those duties.[184] The popular couple would be instrumental in the development of Forest Ranch for years to come.

Berdan's house was becoming a popular resort and was considered headquarters for the upper Butte Creek mines.[185] Ads run in the early part of the decade boasted that the place was newly renovated and furnished.[186] Some of Myron Berdan's neighbors had been treated by the aforementioned Chinese medicine man in Deadwood and convinced the proprietor that it would be nice to have one at his house. So, in 1881, Berdan made plans to have a Chinese physician reside there and establish a hospital;[187] however, it is unclear how long that arrangement lasted.

The hotel, post office and public school kept the West Branch stage stop active during this decade,[188] although things must have been fairly uneventful at times, as an account of three teamsters arriving at the watering trough at the same time became a newsworthy event.[189] At the end of the decade, a large fire burning nearby, supposedly started by herders or campers, must have caused considerable excitement for the residents of this community. A newspaper reported that the intensity of the blaze could have been mitigated if the timber cutters piled their brush in accordance with the law.[190]

1880s: The Road Charter Expires

Speaking of fire, in 1882, the Lomo House, now owned by Alex Cooley, was destroyed by a blaze that appeared to originate in a stovepipe. Although it was not covered by insurance, Mr. Cooley wasted no time rebuilding the old stand along the road,[191] which was the final rest stop before the long pull-up to Little Summit. It didn't last long, however, as the Lomo House, then owned by Mrs. Cooley, burned down once more in 1885. Again, a defective flue was to blame. Although it was covered by insurance this time, the coverage came up about $1,000 short of the estimated damage.[192]

During this decade, the Sutton House went through a series of ownership and management changes. H.T Shirley,[193] Carl Lemm,[194] W.N. Messer,[195] E.K. Brightman and wife,[196] J.M. Barnard,[197] J.E. Carter and Ike Spencer each owned, leased and/or managed the well-known resort at one time or another. Throughout this period, the lively dancing tradition carried on, and people sometimes traveled as much as twenty to thirty miles to attend the merry gatherings. Before her husband took

Lomo Hotel, circa 1880. *Courtesy of CSU, Chico, Meriam Library, Special Collections.*

over the Sutton House, Mrs. Barnard opened a small variety store across from the hotel that sold groceries, stationery, toiletries, fishing tackle and more.[198] In 1888, the seemingly inevitable happened. The hotel, then belonging to the estate of the late J.E. Carter but being leased by Ike Spencer, burned down once more.[199]

During the 1880s, the Butte Meadow House was beginning to establish itself as another popular resort in the Butte Meadows area. Formerly known as the Dodge House, W.C. Roberts was leasing it early in the decade[200] before P.H. Dodge owned and operated it for a while.[201] Mr. Spencer (possibly the same man as in the previous paragraph) managed it for a time after that.[202] Eventually, James McGann took ownership, and in 1889, a flue fire took down this home too.[203] It was not long before the news reported that McGann and his wife were doing a lively business there once more.[204] (James McGann was well known in these parts, mainly because of his work as a civil engineer and Butte County surveyor. He compiled the 1877 and 1886 official maps of Butte County.)[205]

The mineral springs located between the Sutton House and Butte Meadows, purported to have curative properties, were now owned by T.F. Davis. New cottages with amenities were erected, and the place was referred to as Bakerville.[206]

There was not a lot written in the papers about Jonesville during this decade. It appears that its role as a highly popular resort may have diminished somewhat, while the Butte Meadows area was getting most of the attention in the news. In 1884, Jacob Franklin Sims was granted a homestead certification for 160 acres surrounding the town of Jonesville. Later in the decade, Sims sold the acreage to J.F. Dunn.

On the other side of the summit, Mike Bruce's place, the second tollgate, was a breakfast station for stages. Situated in lush, grassy meadows with high-timbered ridges looming above, it was reported to be about forty-eight miles from Chico and seventeen miles from Prattville.[207]

In 1883, John Bidwell's Chico and Humboldt Wagon Road charter finally expired after twenty years. Although he no longer wanted to take full responsibility for keeping the road in good order,[208] Bidwell continued to be highly involved in its management for many years. Transitioning from the wagon road franchise to a public highway was difficult from the start, especially in deciding who was going to maintain the part between Chico and Prattville (sixty-five miles) and determining from where the funding was going to come.

1880s: The Road Charter Expires

To begin with, the road went through several counties (Butte, about forty miles; Tehama, about five miles; and Plumas, about twenty miles),[209] and representatives from the three regions didn't always agree on the best course of action. Furthermore, Tehama County did not feel obliged to maintain the small section that went through its territory at all.[210] After rejecting new franchise proposals, the Butte County Board of Supervisors decided to award contracts for road maintenance and repair on the part of the road it was responsible for. However, these did not go without controversy, including legality issues and accusations of favoritism from the board in rewarding contracts in the county.[211] From 1886 through 1888, J.H. Shuffleton supervised the maintenance and repair of the entire forty-two-mile portion of the road that was Butte County's responsibility. In 1889, Shuffleton took care of about one-half of that stretch, while C.W. Platt was awarded a contract to maintain the rest.[212]

The Chico division of the Sierra Lumber Company went through some major changes during this decade. Early on, the three lumber mills at the upper end of Big Chico Creek were phased out, and a new mill in Chico Meadows was built to replace them. The change-over officially began in 1881, when the machinery was moved from the Arcade Mill to the newly built lumber plant, aptly named the New Arcade Mill, and a new branch of flume was constructed.[213] Soon after, the Belmont Mill closed, and its men were moved to the new location in Chico Meadows.[214] The Cascade Mill lasted one more year and closed for good at the end of the logging season in 1882, when its machinery was moved to a newly built mill in Big Smoky Creek Canyon[215] (north of Big Chico Creek), referred to by historians as the Smoky Creek Mill. Captain Morrison was in charge of the Cascade Mill when it closed down. This was the same man who turned up in Forest Ranch and took over Bonham's mill later that decade.

In the summer of 1882, the New Arcade Mill was reported to be employing fifty men and averaging about forty-three thousand feet per day. This was not quite as much lumber as the Cascade Mill was producing in its final year of operation, or as many men employed, but the wood cut at the new site was of finer quality.[216]

It was during this decade that Barney Cussick began to make a name for himself in the lumber business around the Chico and Humboldt Wagon Road. By late 1880, it was reported that Barney had a contract to furnish logs for both the Arcade and Belmont Mills.[217] When the New Arcade Mill opened, Barney not only had the log contract,[218] but he also supervised the construction and operation of this new mill in Chico Meadows. Furthermore,

Lumber stack ready to be flumed from the New Arcade Mill. *Courtesy of CSU, Chico, Meriam Library, Special Collections.*

Barney built and supervised the Smoky Creek Mill, working under another contract. In 1884, he became Sierra Lumber's mountain manager.

Barney Cussick was probably the most well-known name in the local lumber business during this decade. He acted as a mountain ambassador to the valley, showing visitors around and always keeping the press informed about mill activities. Barney's friendly and outgoing personality served him well after he got out of the lumber business, too, as he eventually became a prominent citizen and a highly successful businessman in Chico.

It was Barney Cussick who first started using stationary steam-powered hoisting equipment in this region during the earlier part of the decade. This mode of energy was used with tramways (light railways) to deliver logs to the mills. (One was reported to go from Butte Meadows to the New Arcade Mill in Chico Meadows.) The Smoky Creek Mill, which cut about fifty thousand feet a day, also used a tramway with stationary steam power to transport lumber to the flume in Big Chico Creek Canyon.[219] Steam donkeys (portable logging engines) were introduced to this part of the country later in the decade to modernize the industry even more. Log chutes (wooden troughs made of peeled tree trunks used to slide logs during transportation) were employed extensively in this area, and the power from beasts of burden was still being used to move logs around.

1880s: The Road Charter Expires

Hoist house for transporting logs over the small ridge between Butte Meadows and the New Arcade Mill. *Courtesy of CSU, Chico, Meriam Library, Special Collections.*

The V-flume down the canyon could still be a perilous place. Luckily, there appeared to be only one death on the waterway during this decade, when Dock Apperson, a flume carpenter, fell almost twenty feet and hit his head on some hard rock below.[220] There were plenty of less serious accidents, however, including some on flume rafts mentioned later on in this chapter. Other injuries occurred by falling from the flume walkway[221] or getting a hand crunched by moving lumber.[222]

Logging injuries at the mountain mills were periodically reported in the paper as well. Although tools—especially wayward axes—were known to injure people,[223] there were two separate incidents in which a worker was killed by a rolling log[224] and two more in which a death resulted from an out-of-control wagon pulled by horses.[225] One man was killed by falling beneath the wheels of a car loaded with logs on a tramway.[226]

In 1881, telegraph instruments along the flume were replaced by telephones.[227] This likely made it much easier to report injuries and request help, since a special skill was no longer required.

Logs being transported down a chute near Butte Meadows, circa 1885. *Courtesy of CSU, Chico, Meriam Library, Special Collections.*

Concerns about destructive logging practices and rainfall distribution were still in the news.[228] In 1885, John Bidwell claimed that the water in Big Chico Creek was decreasing over time due to heavy logging around the sources of the creek, which was denying Rancho Chico an adequate amount of water during the summer months for irrigation, not to mention his flour mill that was set up for water power. Bidwell recognized that forests had a great influence on the amount of moisture in a given district,[229] suggesting he was aware that massive tree removal would impact local climate.

One other lumber mill of note was located along Butte Creek a few miles off Bidwell's road, northeast of Lomo. It was operated by Tickner, Burnham and Company, owners of a well-known variety store in Chico called the White House. Erected in 1882, it was estimated that the portable sawmill would operate for about three years before moving on.[230] As if right on schedule, the mill burned down, along with a blacksmith shop and other buildings, three years later. It was only partially insured.[231]

1880s: The Road Charter Expires

HARROWING SNOW STORIES

Although people often referred to it as "the beautiful" in those days, snow presented obstacles and inconveniences that cannot be entirely understood today with our modern snowplows, snowmobiles and four-wheel-drive vehicles that are often able to move about in the white stuff with such ease. (One disadvantage of living high up in snow country back then was that by late spring, mountain residents often went for long periods without certain luxuries, such as fresh vegetables and fruit, items that were taken for granted in the valley.)[232] Due to the circumstances, people often did things that might seem incomprehensible by today's standards. In the 1880s, the news was not short of stories about the difficulties of getting around in these conditions.

By mid-May 1880, the Sutton House was still snowed in. The only teams that were able to make it that far were those with the mail sleigh. Most supplies had to be delivered on snowshoes from Lomo, six miles away on the other side of the Little Summit. If people wanted to get to the Sutton House for a social gathering, they had to earn it. Although the sleigh was one option, if available, many forged through on snowshoes. In June, the snow was reported to still be as much as seventeen feet at the Big Summit.[233]

Later that year during the following snow season, inclement weather led to tragic consequences for a man who placed the welfare of others ahead of his own. Back then, doctors often made house calls and consequently spent a lot of time on the road, sometimes in harsh conditions. Dr. Joseph Wayland was one of these physicians and ultimately paid the price for it, as reported by the December 21, 1880 *Chico Semi-Weekly Enterprise*:

> *It is with feelings of deep sorrow that we are compelled to announce the death of Dr. Joseph Franklin Wayland, and [sic] old and respected citizen of Chico. About ten days ago he was seized with a severe cold, which was contracted in the discharge of his duty as a physician. A summons came from the mountains for a physician, but owing to the severity of the weather, no one would venture but Dr. Wayland, who set out. He went in his buggy as far as the Lomo House, where he was obliged to go six miles further on horseback, in the midst of a blinding snow storm. On his return he grew rapidly worse, and in spite of all help he died this morning shortly after twelve.*

During that same month, the Chico and Prattville stage, with driver Billy Balch, ran into problems of its own with the weather. The January 1, 1881

Weekly Butte Record described Balch's experience as follows (although the story was taken from a weekly paper published on Saturdays, it was apparently a reprint of a story that was originally reported on the previous Thursday):

> *Balch left Chico one week ago this morning with the intention of going through to Prattville, leaving his stage at Butte Meadows and making the remainder of the trip in a sleigh to which he drives two horses, having them hitched in tandem. He left Butte Meadows on Friday for Prattville. Three days were consumed before the summit was reached. Late Sunday evening one of his horses broke a snow shoe, which compelled the party to remain in the snow all night. At this point the snow was found to be about twenty feet deep. The horses were tied to the sleigh in the road, covered with blankets and made as comfortable as possible, while the men shovelled [sic] a pit in the snow and after considerable difficulty started a fire, around which they spent the night, in a manner that was far more romantic than pleasant. The next morning the snowshoe was repaired, and Prattville was reached late the next evening. On the eastern slope the snow was found to be of less depth and the road better broken. The return trip was made with less difficulty.*

Speaking of snowshoes for horses, until this point, we have only guessed what they looked like, but no longer. The January 8, 1881 *Weekly Butte Record* described these implements for equestrian snow travel in detail: "The stage over the Humboldt road will go through to Prattville, the mail and passengers being transferred to a sleigh at Butte Meadows. The horses attached to the sleigh are hitched in tandem, and make their way over the snow on snow shoes, which are pieces of hard wood, one inch thick and fourteen inches square, and attached to the bottom of the foot by means of iron clasps. The horses readily learn to use their feet with this harness, and with it are enabled to pass over the snow when they would otherwise break through."

Even horses equipped with snowshoes and pulling sleighs over the snow weren't always enough. Sometimes the mail carrier himself had to wear snowshoes and pack the mail over the summit. The February 25, 1882 *Weekly Butte Record* described what Henry Bennet, who was responsible for the section of the road between the Sutton House and Prattville, had to deal with:

> *He has to carry the mail from the Sutton House to Prattville, a distance of thirty miles, on snow shoes, the snow on the road being at present nearly ten feet deep. Bennet has many hardships to endure. At this time there is danger*

1880s: The Road Charter Expires

of encountering on the way some ravenous beast that has been penned up in its den for several days, but is compelled to go forth in search of food, and as the carrier cannot well take with him any weapons of defence [sic], *he would indeed be in a bad predicament should he meet one of these animals; and then again he is likely to get lost on his lonely trip, or be buried in some fearful avalanche of snow sliding down the hillside. Bennet is a plucky fellow and fears nothing, and is surely the man for the position he has. We have heard him tell of the many fearful nights he has spent alone in the mountains in the winter while carrying the mail. At one time a few years since he became tired about half-way on his journey, and was compelled to camp over night on the road. It was fearfully cold, and it would be folly to attempt to pass the night without some shelter. The snow was then about ten feet deep, and the air seemed to indicate that there would be another fall. He knew the warmth of snow beneath its surface, and was confident that if he could dig a hole a few feet under it he could pass the night quite snugly. Using one of his long snow runners as a shovel, he set to work, and in about an hour had a hole large enough to admit himself and mail into a huge drift. He spent that night and half of the next day in his snow cave, and suffered considerably from the pangs of hunger, being without a morsel of food. He did not feel like pushing forward on his way, and was about*

Horses could get around fairly well with specially made snowshoes. Photos taken somewhere in Plumas County. *Courtesy of CSU, Chico, Meriam Library, Special Collections.*

to resign himself to fate when a couple of friends happened to come up, on their way to Prattville from Chico. They had with them a good supply of food and a flask of fine brandy, and it is needless to say that our friend Bennet was soon himself again.

Almost predictably, about a month later, the paper printed another story of the mail carrier between Sutton House and Prattville (this time referred to as Henry Benner but likely the same man as in the previous paragraph) getting stranded in the snow and almost perishing before a search party located him. It was reported that he was revived by a "long and strong 'pull' at a brandy flask."[234]

In February 1887, an unusually heavy snowstorm—one of the worst in memory—struck the foothills. A home and several barns caved in from the weight of the snow, and as a result, a number of horses in those barns became helpless fatalities.[235]

Buck Barham nearly died when he got stranded in the snow. Buck had been working at the Dix Mine in Butte Creek Canyon. It appears that he was attempting to get from there to C.M. Platt's house, where he was living at the time. The house was only about two miles from the mine, but the conditions made it seem a lot farther. The February 11, 1887 *Chico Enterprise* covered the ordeal:

The snow was about four feet deep, and entirely obliterated the trail, but he thought he knew the way so well that he would have no difficulty. In this, however, he was mistaken, for he got lost in the snow, and when darkness came on he was entirely bewildered. After wandering on and on, he finally laid down in despair and gave up. He yelled and halloed [sic], but no assistance came. It was afterwards discovered that he was within a quarter of a mile of the Platt house when he laid down in the snow; and his cries were heard by Mr. Platt, who mistook them for those of a panther. He never thought that they were those of a man, and hence paid no attention to them. On Sunday afternoon, however, Buck varied his cries by calling his wife's name. Then it was realized that the noise could not be made by a panther, and Mr. Platt and others at once went out to investigate.

Late Sunday afternoon, Buck was found, after he had lain in the snow for two days and a night. He was frozen stiff, was out of his senses, his eyes were sunken in his head, and those who discovered him thought he would die. He was at once carried to the Platt place and restoratives applied. In time he recovered his senses, but his legs and the lower part of his body were so badly frozen that nothing could be done for them. His feet and the lower part of his legs had turned black.

Another clipping in the same paper reported that Buck was expected to live. However, the likelihood of keeping all of his toes did not look promising, and his feet were also in danger.

This same snowstorm proved to be quite challenging for Sierra Lumber Company's manager Barney Cussick, thirteen of his employees, twenty-seven horses and eight oxen, who were attempting to escape the mountains for the safety of Chico. The venture took them nearly a week, covering a distance of about thirty-five miles. The February 11, 1887 *Chico Enterprise* also shared this story with its readers (note that Barney's last name was often misspelled by the papers in those days):

Mr. Cusick says that they started out from the Sutton House last Saturday morning at eight o'clock. The snow was then six feet deep, and they traveled all day in a blinding storm. Twenty-two inches more fell during Saturday and Saturday night. The snow being all fresh, the party had the greatest difficulty in getting through it. They did not reach West Branch, only ten miles from their starting point, until three o'clock Sunday morning. Before that time some of the men were nearly frozen and were constantly falling asleep in their saddles from the excessive cold. It required the constant exertions of the others to keep them from giving up altogether, and Mr. Cusick says that many times during the first day's trip he despaired of ever reaching Chico with all his party alive.

The rest of the journey was but a repetition of this first day. The party came right down the Humboldt road, making but a few miles each day and fighting every step of the way. They could not stop or go back, because the stock just about exhausted the feed at each place where they stayed over night, and this compelled the party to push on. To make a trail for the stock, some of the men were compelled to crawl ahead on their hands and knees, or flat on their stomachs, in order to beat down the snow. Frequently a man would sink in the soft snow up to his neck, and would have to be drawn out by his companions, by main force. The horses and oxen would follow in single file in the trail made by the men, but often they would attempt to go side by side, only to sink down and have to be hauled out by the men.

The journey was one continued struggle, and full of hardships and suffering. That all the party arrived alive and without the loss of any of

In the business for quite some time, it's likely that many of the vehicles made in Canfield's Carriage Shop were used on the Humboldt Wagon Road. *Chico Daily Enterprise* ad dated February 2, 1889.

the stock, is considered remarkable. They were thankful enough to reach Chico after their disagreeable experiences, and the opinion of all is probably expressed in the remark of one who said: "I would not take the trip again for a stack of twenty dollar pieces three feet high."

Another mail carrier between the Sutton House and Prattville made the news later that month. A man named Murphy was making the trip over the mountains on snowshoes when he was delayed by the nasty weather and was feared lost when he did not arrive at his destination as scheduled.[236] Murphy eventually showed up safe and sound but suffered some snow blindness and gave up the job.[237]

Even attempted robberies occurred in the snow. Johnny Veal, a veteran "whip," had a narrow escape near the Big Summit one day, using his wits to outsmart his would-be assailant. Johnny was carrying the mail in a large sleigh that was manufactured at Canfield's shop in Chico. The January 17, 1888 *Chico Daily Enterprise* told it this way, although the paper spelled Veal's first name differently than usual spellings:

> After leaving the Sutton House, when near the Big Summit, a man stepped out from behind a small clump of trees and asked for a ride, and as the fellow had a rifle and looked wicked Johnnie complied with the demand. The fellow proved to be a rough ungainly fellow and eyed Johnnie's gold watch and the mail bags in a very suspicious manner. Johnnie grew apprehensive and any move he would make toward the bottom of the sleigh where his shooting irons lay, would cause the stranger to tightly grasp his rifle and look daggers at the driver. After racking his brain for an excuse of ridding himself of his unwelcome customer, Johnnie hit on the following: When near a curve in

the road he lashed his horses, and when they became almost unmanageable accidently knocked his hat off. He politely asked the man to get it for him and the fellow climbed out, but took his rifle with him. Just as soon as he turned the corner, Veal whipped the animals into a run and was just turning another curve when the baffled robber appeared and sent a flying shot after him. It went wide of its mark though and Johnnie glided safely into Prattville. A search party was organized, but nothing was found of the man. Veal returned home Saturday, and is thankful over his lucky escape.

MINING FOR GOLD WAS NO HOLIDAY

In the 1880s, a number of drift mines were operating along the West Branch of Butte Creek, just east of Berdan's. The men who worked these mines bored their way through the canyon walls like human moles, tunneling in sometimes as far as three hundred to six hundred feet,[238] to reach gold-bearing gravels of an ancient river channel that flowed during the Tertiary Period of the geologic time scale. By the time gold-seekers arrived, some of this old, dried-up waterway had been exposed where the West Branch of Butte Creek had cut through the overlying volcanic Tuscan Formation, but most of the dead river's treasures were still buried deep in the earth. Using tools of the trade, extracted drift material was loaded into rail carts and then taken out to the water for washing and separating the gold.

The work wasn't easy, but it paid off for the few enterprising prospectors who were willing to work hard. In 1885, a nugget weighing thirteen ounces was pulled out of a claim located somewhere along the West Branch of Butte Creek.[239] During the 1880s, gold was going for around $20 per troy ounce, and Scribner and Wiseman were digging out quite a bit of the precious metal on Portuguese Point. In 1881, they collected more than $1,800 worth of gold in three weeks,[240] and in 1885, it was reported that the mine was still producing well.

In 1885, the John Dix claim, a little downstream, reportedly came up with a piece of gold worth $800,[241] and in 1887, it was noted in the paper that the highly successful Dix Mine made a regular contribution to Butte County's wealth.[242] In 1885, three men were each taking out $100 a week by drifting the Garland claim.[243] There were reports of other claims having good success as well. Of course, miners were also known for keeping some of their finds a secret, so some good strikes likely went unreported.

Miners at work in a tunnel. *From* Hutchings' California Magazine, *July 1857.*

This kind of work was only appropriate for a rugged type of individual—one who was willing to put up with some discomfort. The April 22, 1881 *Chico Semi-Weekly Enterprise* explained what the boys from the West Branch of Butte Creek at Portuguese Point had to contend with: "The pluck displayed by these hardy 'miner boys' when they start in to unearth 'a mine of wealth' is quite surprising to a novice, and they are pre-eminently deserving of the rich rewards they often secure. Handling a pick, sledge, gad and shovel in a dripping tunnel or drift, is no holiday amusement either, for the boys often come forth, at the close of a day's labor, as wet as a mouse in a pan of milk."

THE RACQUETTE

As mentioned earlier, the Sutton House was the venue for quite a few lively dance parties throughout the decade. One new dance that the hotel featured, called the "racquette," was described in the July 1, 1881 *Chico Semi-Weekly Enterprise*:

> *The lady and gentleman stand facing each other, quite close together. The gentleman's right arm is delicately placed around the lady's waist, his left hand clutching her index finger, while her left hand is placed on his right shoulder. Finally the fiddles, after a few see-saws, strike up: "A dog ate a rye-straw, rye-straw; a dog ate a rye-straw, rye-straw," etc. At the sound of*

1880s: The Road Charter Expires

Dance pavilion at Butte Meadows, circa 1903. *Courtesy of CSU, Chico, Meriam Library, Special Collections.*

"dog" the dancers jump off to the gentleman's left two jumps, as though the dog were biting them from the rear, and they in their efforts to escape were trying to dodge past each other but couldn't. After two jumps to the lady's left they both halt an instant with their feet about fifteen inches apart and bending the knees inward toward each other until they nearly touched. We could only see the gentleman's knees, but we suppose the lady did the same; then both suddenly spring one jump to the lady's left, and thus backward and forward, keeping their knees rigidly in the above position all the time, but with limber knees and hip joints they make a graceful swinging motion up and down to the time of the music. When the music stops a moment the dancers stop, and then at the sound of "dog" they both swing off again, and repeat the maneuvre [sic] over and over, until both become exhausted, the fiddles stop, and they sink into seats in a perfect perspiration of rapture. That's the racquette.

Dashing through the Snow

Although the West Branch way station did not appear to get as much news coverage as other mountain communities during this decade, at least Harry Sharp provided enough material one day to warrant an entertaining story. The March 24, 1882 *Chico Semi-Weekly Enterprise* reported the incident as follows:

> *We hear great commiseration expressed by some of our valley people for the "poor people in the mountains," surrounded by snow-banks. A letter received this week tells us that the people up in the snow beds are enjoying themselves in first-rate style, and have their sleigh-rides and dancing parties as usual. Lately a party took place at the West Branch and Harry Sharp, the noted ladies-man of the Humboldt road, rigged up a sleigh for the occasion, and loaded it with the sweetest morsels of femininity to be found in Butte county. The girls had spent considerable time fixing their bangs and frills and were looking charming. Harry, too, felt good over his company, and whipped up his team with a proud consciousness of the responsibility he had in his load. Away they went over the snow, and the jingling sleigh bells and merry laugh mingled together in sweet cadence. Everything was lovely, and the full realization of happiness had been reached when suddenly something in the snow seemed to give way, the sleigh went up on one side and down on the other—in plain English there was an upset, and Harry's whole load was dumped unceremoniously out. Harry held to the lines and prevented a runaway. There was a momentary shrieking of the girls, but they all managed to right themselves in good condition. Harry was sorry he could not help them, but he had his hands full with the horses. Our correspondent describes the scene in the snow as rich, the snow was discolored by the paint and powder from the girls' faces....*

Luckily, nobody was seriously injured—just a few scratches. However, the girls were reported to have given Harry "fits" ever since.

Dead Man's Hill

Dead Man's Hill was sometimes referred to as Dead Man's Grade. Either way, with a name like that, one would suspect that something bad happened there, and indeed, that was the case. It turns out that the hill earned its dreadful name thanks to one gruesome incident in which a man was found lying in the road, robbed and brutally mutilated.[244] The slope with the unpleasant title, located about twelve miles from Chico,[245] managed to inspire a few stories in the press during the early 1880s.

George Robinson let his wagonload of lumber slide into a deep chuckhole on the grade, causing it to upset and break the reach in two.[246] Mr. McKnight was hauling a heavy load of lumber down the Chico and Humboldt Wagon Road when, near the grade at Dead Man's Hill, the harness of one of the wheel horses gave way, and the ten-horse team bolted. As the lumber slid forward and passed over a stumbling wheel horse, the panicked team continued on for a way, dragging along the severely injured animal and the compromised load.[247]

Probably the worst accident occurred one day when a teamster named Bernard was going to Chico with a huge load of lumber and a ten-horse team. The July 8, 1882 *Weekly Butte Record* described the horrifying accident: "As he was turning a sharp curve on the grade, the brake-block on the wagon broke, throwing the horses, the driver and the load into a canyon several hundred feet below. Seven of the horses were instantly killed and three escaped with serious injuries. Bernard had one of his legs broken and sustained several severe bruises."

It seems that equines, in particular, were at high risk along this section of the road. In fact, the grade could just as well have been called Dead Horse Hill.

Dead Man's Hill was also the location of a stage robbery early in the decade. Two men and a boy held up W.N. Messer's eastbound stage, driven by Ed. Nelson, with three passengers aboard. The stage was about to go on the grade when the highwaymen stepped out from their hiding places and ordered Nelson to stop. It was reported earlier that the driver was relieved of his watch and chain,[248] but a week later, the June 2, 1882 *Chico Enterprise* gave an amended version of the events:

> It appears that Nelson was not molested at all, but the robbers ordered him to come down off his box and stand by the head of his leaders. This he did, managing while so standing to slip his purse containing $70 in gold from his pocket to the inside of his drawers, but even this was unnecessary, as they did not ask him for anything. James Craig threw his purse with $35 in gold into a bush, and came back and got it, but had to give up some seven or eight dollars which he had loose in his pocket. They did not molest Mrs. Messer. Johnny Wilson was the

Stage robbery, drawn by R.F. Zogbaum. *From Coy's 1925 book,* Pictorial History of California.

other passenger on board, and he tried to make friends with the robbers. He had a bottle of whiskey and asked them all to take a drink, which they refused. He pressed them hard, telling them to be sociable. But they said they wanted to first get through with the job they had on hand. They relieved Johnny of his loose coin, some ten or twelve dollars and his watch and chain, worth, probably, one hundred dollars. They then allowed the stage to depart, while they went over the hill. After going a short distance the stage was stopped and Craig returned and found his purse all right. Fortunately he had forgot his watch, a very valuable one, on leaving his home in Chico, or it also would have gone.

The *Weekly Butte Record* noted that the robbers seemed nervous and inexperienced.[249] Maybe the friendly Johnny Wilson was just trying to calm their nerves a bit by offering them a snort or two of whiskey, but it seems more likely he had another plan in mind.

1880s: The Road Charter Expires

BILLY BONESS STILL IN THE NEWS

Near the Ten-Mile House, Billy Boness and his hunting exploits continued to make the news.[250] One newspaper noted that he probably killed more wild animals than any other man in the area.[251] Billy once killed a huge mountain lion that was eventually stuffed and put on public exhibition for a couple of days, prompting the editor of the March 16, 1883 *Chico Enterprise* to remark, "The grizzly bear and the California lion, two of the great beasts of this coast, are rapidly disappearing, and will soon be seen only as this one is, in places where curiosities are kept."

Although the latter species was able to escape this grim fate—barely— the editor was quite prophetic about the former. The California brown, or grizzly, bear once frequently seen roaming in the valley and mountains of the state was hunted to extinction by the early twentieth century. California's state animal can still be seen on its flag and official seal.

Returning to Mr. Boness, we know he was pretty tough on wild beasts; however, Billy didn't appear to strike as much fear in some humans. In 1880,

Both black and brown bears were hunted, and the cubs were fair game. Drawing by nineteenth-century artist F.O.C. Darley, titled *After a Day's Sport in the Sierras*.

he went on trial for drawing a pistol on William Bruce but was let off for what Boness called an act of self-defense after being continually harassed and threatened by the man. Bruce was fined ten dollars for disturbing the peace.[252]

In 1883, Billy was relieved of a watch, revolver and twenty dollars by a robber along Butte Creek.[253] It only goes to show that, for some people, two-footed animals can be more troublesome than the four-footed kind.

Scary Bear Stories

Billy Boness knew how to handle bears, but not every encounter with a big bruin along the Humboldt Road during the 1880s went as well as it did for Billy.

G.W. Colby was hunting around the Butte Meadows area one late afternoon and managed to bag a good-sized bear. The news reported that, while basking in the glory of his kill, he suddenly heard some ferocious growls from behind and turned to see the mate of the bruin charging right at him from about ten feet away. The frightened man who abruptly went from being the hunter to the hunted managed to escape by swiftly climbing up a small tree. Colby ended up staying the night and part of the next day perched high in his uncomfortable seat while the angry beast camped below, just waiting for the treed human to make a mistake. Eventually, something frightened the bear, and it ran off. Colby managed to survive the ordeal, although it was said that after that experience, he switched to looking for smaller game.[254] (Although black bears are quite adept at climbing trees, adult grizzlies are not generally known to do the same, as their big, heavy bodies make it too difficult.)

Mr. Epperson of Forest Ranch had a good scare one day. Apparently, a bear and her cub were scrounging around in the blackberry patch on his property when some hunters who were camped in the neighborhood took the opportunity to shoot the cub while it was roaming on its own. When the old bear noted her loss, she went crazy, bristling with fury and howling up a storm. Epperson came out of his house to see what all the commotion was about, and when the enraged bear saw the curious resident, she went after him, chasing Epperson back indoors, where he ended up staying for some time.[255]

Although most people in those days used guns to kill bears, Fred Kingsbury showed that there was another way that could be just as effective. However, his technique was not recommended for anyone with any common sense unless it became absolutely necessary, which, apparently, in this case, it was. The August 22, 1884 *Chico Enterprise* told how it was done:

> *The early part of last week Fred Kingsbury, who resides in the mountains near Butte Meadows, went out one morning to mend some fence which had become dilapidated. For company he took his two dogs along with him, and while at work he heard them barking loudly, and going to see what was the matter, he found that they had bayed a large brown bear. Bruin and the dogs were having a fierce contest; Mr. Kingsbury had no weapon with him but the ax, with which he prepared to defend himself. When Bruin saw the gentleman he came after him, and just as he was about to make a lunge, Fred, who has a "hey like a heagle," wielded his ax with perfect precision and clave old Bruin's skull in twain, cutting through the brain in the single blow. Fred went and got some help, they dressed the bear, and have had "bar" meat for breakfast every day since.*

Sometimes It Was Better to Walk

Stage upsets occasionally happened on the Humboldt Road. One time, near Forest Ranch, driver Johnny Veal pulled over to let some opposing traffic slip by. The problem was that he got too far out on the bank, and over he went, along with his six lady passengers and a number of men on their way to work at the mills. No one was injured.[256]

On the Big Summit, driver Wash Boyer showed how snow could cause a vehicle to end up on its side, as explained in the June 11, 1886 *Chico Enterprise*:

> *The road between Chico and Prattville is in tolerable condition, except for a distance of about five hundred yards on the summit, where the snow has not yet melted. Last week the stage was overturned at this point. It was the trip when Mr. and Mrs. Chas. Woods, Miss Molly Camper, and several others from Chico were aboard. All of the party had got out to walk over the bad part of the road, except Wash Boyer, the driver, and Mrs. Woods. When the accident occurred Mrs. Woods was thrown out, but, luckily for her, she landed in a snow bank and was not hurt at all. Wash Boyer lit in the road and was considerably shaken up; but the event on the whole was not serious, and only served to furnish amusement for the others, who were very glad they had chosen to walk.*

Wash Boyer had a rough time of it on occasion. Once a stump knocked him off his perch on the stage, and he hit the ground with his head.[257] Another time, he was on a buckboard with three passengers when a boulder that rolled onto the road threw him from his seat, and he suffered another head injury.[258] No one ever said being a driver on the Humboldt Road was easy.

FRANK MICKEY'S WILD RIDE

Wagon accidents could happen anywhere, anytime, on the Humboldt Road, but it wasn't too often that kids got in on the action. However, one afternoon, some children near Forest Ranch created a worrisome situation. The May 20, 1887 *Chico Enterprise* passed this story along:

> *Yesterday afternoon about half-past three o'clock, Frank Mickey was coming down the grade just above Forest Ranch, with a load of furniture and household goods. Some children coming from school overtook him and climbed on his wagon for a ride. On the way down the steep grade the horses began to kick and became unmanageable. Mickey had his left arm around a little girl, trying to hold her on, and with the other arm was endeavoring to hold*

Dr. Oscar Stansbury (*right*) camping at Butte Meadows, circa 1890. *Courtesy of CSU, Chico, Meriam Library, Special Collections.*

the horses. Suddenly the brake gave way and he was thrown forward, down under the horses' feet. The little girl, whose name was Isadore Knight, fell off on one side to the ground and broke her right arm between the elbow and shoulder. Mickey was kicked by one of the horses just over his left eye, and quite a gash was cut by the horse's hoof. The wagon also passed over his back, bruising him badly. The accident occurred near Forest Ranch and was witnessed by several men, who at once ran to the scene, picked up the little girl and helped Mickey home. A man was immediately dispatched to Chico for Dr. O. Stansbury, who went up last night and set the little girl's arm. Mickey's injuries were not serious, and he is up and around again to-day.

A Christmas Miracle

The following is a heartwarming story that could have turned out tragically. But this is a Christmas story, so it's only appropriate that it had a happy ending. The December 30, 1887 *Chico Enterprise* explained:

On Christmas day an accident occurred at Forest Ranch, which for its lucky results reflects credit on the bravery of a gallant young man and saved a young lady from meeting a terrible death by being dashed on the rocks, two hundred feet below, in Chico Canyon. Sunday afternoon, a party of young ladies and gentlemen from Chico, who were visiting friends at Forest Ranch were out on the bluffs just above the house, and among them was a young Eastern lady, Miss Nona Ratcliff, of Greenville, Ohio. They were standing on the edge of the bluff, which at this place is about two hundred feet high and from where they shelved outward and down for about thirty feet, and then abruptly broke into a perpendicular fall to the bottom of the canyon. Miss Ratcliff was out on the extreme edge peering over when her foothold gave way, she grasped the edge of the rocks but could not stop herself, and began rapidly falling to what her companions thought a terrible death. She rolled as far as the shelf of rocks when her dress caught, and she hung there over the yawning gulf almost two hundred feet below, expecting death at every moment. Her companions who were much frightened at once realized her alarming position, and the thought of saving her quickly entered their minds. Dispatching one of the young men to the house for a rope, Mr. Henry Epperson took off his coat and slowly and cautiously made his way to where the young lady lay. She was pulled from the edge of the bluff, and when the rope came was taken to the top and home. Miss Ratcliff suffered a sprained ankle, her arm was badly wrenched, and she was otherwise bruised. The rescue was a brave and fortunate one, and we congratulate all parties on the escape from a horrible death.

Shootout Near the Big Summit

Henry C. Hill was about thirty years old and lived most of his life in Los Angeles County and Sacramento. He was described as a slight built man of 120 pounds with a weak face, grey eyes, small chin and a shifting, restless look. In the summer of 1889, he worked on a ranch in Oak Grove near Sacramento. He left Sacramento to find work in the mountains with a poorly thought-out plan that if he failed to find work there, he would try his hand at stage robbing. After not having any luck finding a job, he wandered around a few days until finally arriving at Mapes's ranch, just north of Honey Lake in Lassen County, where he slept in the barn for an evening.

It was near Mapes's where the opportunity to carry out his plan presented itself. The Wells Fargo and Co.'s Fort Bidwell (named in honor of John Bidwell)[259] stage was passing through just north of Mapes's ranch when Mr. Hill held it up and managed to get away with $1,000.

The real excitement began later when Sheriff Frank Cady hunted down the suspect. The lawman began to track the highwayman from the scene of the robbery and followed his trail from Lassen County clear across Plumas County, stopping at places along the way and getting reports from people who had recently seen the fugitive. On his way from Greenville to Prattville, the sheriff talked to a peddler, who told him he had seen a man who fit the description on the Chico road. The sheriff picked up the trail about four miles west of Prattville. At Henry Feiss's place, he took a fresh team, and the chase was on, with Mr. Feiss driving the wagon. Sheriff Cady traced the robber to a point about one and a half miles past the Big Summit where the trail left the road, now in Butte County. We'll let the sheriff describe what happened after that, as told in the September 5, 1889 *Lassen Advocate*, a Susanville paper:

I got out of the wagon and followed it in. As I entered the bushes the sun was just about on a level with the top of the hill (it was about 5 P.M.) and

1880s: The Road Charter Expires

Main Street, Fort Bidwell, circa 1886. The school is on the left and hotel on the right.
Courtesy of CSU, Chico, Meriam Library, Special Collections.

shining directly in my eyes. I had only gone about twenty-five yards, when I saw my man crouching under a bush, with his pistol leveled upon me. I started to tell him to hold up his hands, raising my pistol at the same time, when he fired his shot taking effect in the calf of my right leg. He then rose up and came toward me, firing as he came, his last shot having been fired when he was within twelve feet of me. All this time I was trying to shoot, and succeeded in firing three times, but my pistol had gotten gummed up and foul with my long ride in the dust, and as I had to take both hands to raise the hammer and all my strength to pull it off, so my aim was no good, though I sent one bullet through his leg, making an ugly flesh wound.

    When he came so close, and was just about to pull again, I jumped for him, and we grappled, he throwing both arms about me, ducking his head close under my arm, so that I could not hit him a fair blow. I got in one, however, with the butt of my Smith & Wesson on his head, that sent the blood down over his face and bosom and he cried "I quit!" whereupon I slipped the hand-cuffs on him and led him out to the road, where we sat down and waited for the team, which had taken fright at the firing and had run away during the temporary absence of Mr. Feiss. They were stopped a little way up the grade by a peddler and we were soon on our way down to Feiss' place where we met Mr. Thacker, Wells Fargo & Co's detective, who had also been on the trail. I took an inventory of myself after supper, and found I had received three wounds—one through the calf of my right

Lassen Advocate printing office staff, circa 1890. *Courtesy of CSU, Chico, Meriam Library, Special Collections.*

leg, one through the fleshy part of the thigh and one about three inchgs [sic] *round to the front of the thigh from the second wound, the ball passing down and remaining in the leg.*

The next day, on the way back to Susanville, the prisoner confessed that he hid the money close to where he was captured. Detective Thacker and the robber then went back and recovered the greenbacks while the tired and wounded sheriff continued to Susanville. Hill used a small .32-caliber bulldog pistol to injure the lawman (a shotgun, recovered at an earlier time, was used during the robbery), but none of the wounds proved to be serious.

It was not long before the robber was brought to trial in Susanville. Judge Marsteller sentenced Mr. Hill to serve seventeen years in the state prison at Folsom and told the prisoner he was showing mercy on him, despite the fact that Hill had committed two crimes—the robbery, for which a plea of guilty was entered, and the deadly attack on a sworn officer of the law.

Being rather green at this robbery business, Henry Hill did not have a good escape plan. He was unfamiliar with the mountains, didn't know where he was going and didn't even realize that he was being pursued. Even though

John Bidwell was never directly involved in the events, a stage line linked to the fort named for him was robbed, and the "road agent" was eventually caught on the road he built. Maybe it would have been a wiser plan for Henry to stay away from anything that might be associated with Mr. Bidwell no matter what.

THRILLING V-FLUME RIDES

The 1880s had several exciting Big Chico Creek V-flume riding accidents to report, and no one appeared to die from any of them. Instead, all these men survived to share their amazing stories with others and possibly inspire some to think twice before deciding to embark on a wild ride down the Big Chico Creek V-flume.

On one such occasion, Ike McClusky did the talking for poor Shorty Burk. The March 18, 1882 *Weekly Butte Record* reported:

> *Ike tells a good story on "Shorty" Burk, who started to Chico in the flume the other day for "supplies." "Shorty" built a long raft and started down the V in fine shape, but he was doomed to grief. He was taking everything easy—lying on his back, reading the last number of the* RECORD *and smoking his pipe. In turning a sharp curve in the flume at Cape Horn, his raft separated, spilling Burk out into the chilling snow water. After considerable struggling he grasped the side of the flume and drew himself out, but in trying to walk on its side he slipped and fell head long into a huge snow-drift, from which perilous position he was rescued by a flume-walker.*

An even more spectacular accident occurred about a year later. The April 14, 1883 *Weekly Butte Record* reported, "John Molder, a laborer on the flume, met with a frightful accident at Smoky Flat yesterday. He was coming to Chico in a large pine box, which was heavily loaded, and its weight broke down the flume, throwing him to the ground, a distance of over ninety feet....The flume is getting old and rotten, and each year the danger of riding down its course becomes more dangerous."

Although, amazingly, Molder appeared to have no obvious broken bones, some feared that he may have suffered some internal injuries. The other local newspaper and lack of any death record suggest that he survived the harrowing incident with nothing more than bruises.[260]

An adventurous ride on a V-flume down the eastern slope of the Sierra Nevada Mountains to Huffaker's Station, Nevada, during the 1870s. *Courtesy of Nevada Historical Society.*

1880s: The Road Charter Expires

A.G. "Bert" Mason's story may top the previous two. The September 16, 1887 *Chico Enterprise* described the unfortunate sequence of events as follows:

> *A.G. Mason left the mills at twelve o'clock yesterday on a raft in the flume for a ride to Chico. He expected to make the trip in three and one-half hours, but met with several thrilling mishaps that delayed him until after dark and effectually cured him for a raft ride to Chico. The ride for the first fifteen miles was novel and grand—scenery as magnificent as any in the Sierra Nevadas. But when the raft struck the deep canyons and mountain gorges, with the flume stretched along looking like a silvery thread from the bottom, the ride began to take on dangers, for the lumber that had been shipped in the morning was here met with, and the real trouble commenced. In one of the deep cuts the V box ran on to a huge board, up-ending the raft and throwing Bert high in the air. In falling, he grasped a small board nailed to the flume and hung suspended fifty feet from the bottom of the canyon. Bert, having but one arm, found himself in a dangerous position; and, to add to his horror, the board he was hanging to began to break. About twenty feet below him was a small platform between the joists, so, just as the board gave way, Bert swung out, let go his hold and dropped. He struck the platform, but the rebound threw him thirty feet to the bottom of the canyon, striking on his shoulder and the side of his face. He was stunned for a moment, but when he came to he hurried down the flume and caught the raft. When twelve miles from Chico, he was again thrown, but this time struck in the flume, with a narrow escape from drowning. His hat was lost and he was wet through. As soon as he got out, Bert concluded he did not want any more raft riding, and walked the remaining twelve miles to town, arriving at 7:30. He will return to the mills to-morrow.*

Captain O'Neil rode the flume many times without any significant mishaps. However, his luck ran out one day, and the lumberman barely escaped serious injury, possibly even death. The circumstances were described in the May 10, 1889 *Chico Daily Enterprise*:

> *The Captain was riding from the "Palace" in a box and just before turning a curve he heard a crash ahead of him, which served to put him on his guard, and perhaps to this he owes his escape from a very serious accident. On the "box" rounding the curve, he perceived the cause of the crash to be a large limb which had broken from a tree and fallen directly across the flume. The Captain stood up on the box and made a jump for the sidewalk along*

the edge of the flume; he struck all right, but the board broke throwing the Captain to the ground about twenty feet below. He fortunately landed on soft soil and thereby save [sic] *himself, though badly bruised on the hip and side. We congratulate him on his fortunate escape.*

The Hoisting Works

The Smoky Creek Mill was located in a canyon that was too steep for teams to haul out the lumber, so a steam-powered hoist was used with a tramway to draw lumber cars up and over a ridge and down the other side (forty-five-degree slopes) to the V-flume in Big Chico Creek Canyon. The wire cable was reported to be two and a half miles long, and it wound around a large wooden cylinder located at the top of the ridge. When the whistle blew, the machinery would begin working, and it either drew the cable up or lowered it down. Attached at the other end were two cars, each loaded with about 2,500 feet of lumber.[261] A correspondent for the October 12, 1883 *Chico Enterprise* reminded readers of the danger involved: "The gentleman who is employed as car tender has a very dangerous situation riding back and forth up and down the mountains; for if any piece of machinery should break the car would doubtless go to the destruction and he would probably be hurled into eternity."

Put Your Head in the Hat

Not only did a logger have a rough job, but he also had to be tough at play. The September 4, 1885 *Chico Enterprise* explained how some of the boys had fun in the camps:

> *One of their favorite games is "put your head in the hat." They draw lots and the unfortunate victim hides his face by drawing a hat over it. Somebody gives him a whack with the palm of his hand, and he is required to guess who the man was. If he guesses right he is relieved by the man who gave the blow. As some of the men have a hand like a sledgehammer the unfortunate sometimes gets black and blue before he guesses correctly. The fun is enjoyed intensely by the whacker, although the one who gets whacked may not appreciate the joke so hugely. I have seen them keep up this for two solid hours.*

1880s: The Road Charter Expires

Smoky Creek Mill hoist house, circa 1888. *Courtesy of CSU, Chico, Meriam Library, Special Collections.*

Tragedy Strikes the Cussick Family

In 1888, tragedy struck Barney Cussick and family when the lumberman's five-year-old daughter Maggie passed away from a two-week stomach ailment. By then, the highly regarded logging supervisor was well known throughout the county, and the local press wasted no time offering heartfelt condolences for the bereaved parents.[262] The August 2, 1888 *Chico Daily Enterprise* published a letter from a correspondent in Butte Meadows, which ended with this moving poem:

> *We are waiting, Maggie, waiting,*
> *For the hours to pass away,*
> *When we'll meet to part, no, never,*
> *On the resurrection day.*
>
> *We are waiting, Maggie, waiting,*
> *For that blossom young and fair—*
> *Rudely taken from our bosoms,*
> *Though we nursed it with such care.*
>
> *We are waiting, Maggie, waiting,*
> *Round the little grave so low—*
> *Feeling all our hopes have perished,*
> *With the flower we cherished so.*
>
> *We are waiting, Maggie, waiting,*
> *For the death that is to come—*
> *Though it be a little later,*
> *We shall all be gathered home.*
>
> *We are waiting, Maggie, waiting,*
> *For the voices far away—*
> *If they call us, we are waiting,*
> *Only waiting to obey.*
>
> E.F.

1880s: The Road Charter Expires

THE GOVERNMENT VS. SIERRA LUMBER COMPANY

In early 1886, news came out that the U.S. General Land Office was going to file charges against the Sierra Lumber Company for cutting more than sixty million feet of lumber on government lands in California that were adjacent to the company-owned properties.[263] Apparently this was not an uncommon practice for some lumber companies at the time,[264] since their holdings were often next to lands in public domain that were easily accessible. (It seems one tactic was to file a fraudulent claim on government land; another would be to just cut away at will.) Sierra Lumber admitted that there was large-scale depredation on government land but claimed it was done prior to the organization of its company. The government charged that the cutting occurred between the fall of 1878 and early 1886.[265]

The indictment, which included violations committed in Butte and Tehama Counties, was filed on April 5, 1886,[266] but the suit dragged on for several years, as the government kept postponing the trial. By the end of 1888, the lawsuit finally got underway.[267] The government subpoenaed more than seventy-five witnesses[268] in the high-profile case, but some of their expertise may have been questionable at best. A local paper wrote that the suit was a farce and reported that, early on in the proceedings, one of the special agent witnesses for the plaintiff admitted that until he went to Butte County for the government, he'd never been in a large forest and couldn't tell from a stump the year in which it was cut down.[269] The January 19, 1889 *Chico Daily Enterprise* had this take on the affair:

> *The great suit of the Government against the Sierra Lumber Company, is expected to close in a day or two. This has been a most tedious and expensive suit, and one that we do not believe will amount to anything in the end. The total ignorance of the government agents, of what kind of trees have been cut for lumber and on what sections they were cut, was most marked. One agent on the stand could not tell an oak from a pine, and after he had described the land where the lumber had been cut as government land, the attorney for the Company produced the title-deeds to the same land, which they had owned for years. Had the company been inclined they had plenty opportunity to get easy off, but they preferred to stand a suit, and close up the mouths of blackmailers, who thirsted for bloodmoney* [sic].

The suit came to a close shortly after, with the jury deciding on a settlement of $41,000 and costs for the suit in favor of the government.

(The original amount for damages incurred was reported to be more than $2.1 million.) Sierra Lumber admitted to cutting on government land but claimed that only 1.5 million feet of lumber was involved and that it did so with no fraudulent intent.[270]

The final settlement wasn't made until the next decade. Ultimately, the Sierra Lumber Company paid $15,000.[271] The newspaper was right. The suit did seem like a big waste of time.

4
1890s

Clashing Over Road Maintenance

OVERVIEW

In 1891, Hog Springs appeared to be more than just a water stop. A correspondent traveling the road described a delightful breakfast of cold chicken and hot coffee boiled on a campfire, at what he jokingly referred to as "Hotel de Hog Springs,"[272] possibly referring to bygone times.

Early on, not very much news came out about the Ten-Mile House, except that in 1891, it was reported that Martin Crum, the tavern-keeper, died after being ill for about a week.[273] Water was still hauled up from the canyon below, and in 1895, the news reported that the Ten-Mile House was probably the only place in Northern California that sold water.[274]

In 1891, the *Chico Daily Enterprise* advertised that the Fourteen-Mile House was for rent and to contact Henry and Diller of Chico if interested. It was suggested that the eight-room hotel, barn, corral, small house and acreage, which included a vineyard and orchard, would easily bring in more than the rent.[275] Historical sources indicate that around the middle of the decade, John Lucas, who had previously resided on land just down the road, took over the management of the Fourteen-Mile House establishment and sometime later rebuilt the hotel.

Forest Ranch received quite a bit of attention from the news during this decade, mainly because of its many celebrations and parties that generally included various entertaining activities and great food. The community's

The first Forest Ranch School was in session during the last few decades of the 1800s. *Courtesy of CSU, Chico, Meriam Library, Special Collections.*

literacy society had gatherings and held at least one notable fundraiser with theatrical and musical performances.[276] The school presented programs in which children sometimes dressed up in costumes and acted or sang.[277] Adults and kids attended school picnics that might include activities such as guitar medleys, dialogues, recitals, footraces, tug-of-wars and pie-eating contests.[278] It was reported that during the summer of 1890, the people of Forest Ranch were regularly entertained at parties by delightful music provided by Fred Dorrett on the guitar and Cash Crum on the violin.[279]

Of course, holidays were recognized in the small, wooded community too. An annual Mayday picnic was once celebrated with a literary program, tasty food, the usual games and a dance.[280] Decoration Day (now Memorial Day) was once honored with the raising of the flag, recitals, songs, stories and speeches.[281] Washington's Birthday (now Presidents' Day) was recognized, although it appears a contingent from Forest Ranch traditionally went to Chico to observe the ceremonies unless the weather dictated otherwise.[282] Christmas was a special occasion, and in addition to decorations, presents and other pleasurable activities, a turkey shoot might be part of the entertainment.[283]

Captain and Mrs. Morrison were known to be good hosts at the Forest Ranch hotel. The proximity of Forest Ranch to the valley, and its cooler foothill temperatures, attracted quite a few people from below for short vacations. In 1891, Captain Morrison completed a new sawmill.[284] Although the mill was not particularly large—in 1893, it was reported to employ only eight men—it was nonetheless a boost to the local economy. It offered owners of small ranches a supplemental income.[285]

Captain Morrison was a busy man. In 1893, he bought the stock and wagons from the insolvent estate of Johnny Veal and formed a new stage company to run between Chico and Prattville and Chico and Powellton. (Although Powellton was on the Humbug Road, it could be reached from Chico via a road that went through Butte Creek Canyon.) Johnny Veal wasn't out of work. He still managed the company.[286]

J.H. Shuffleton's place in Forest Ranch was also getting some attention in the press. The foothill orchard was becoming a prosperous industry and demonstrated once again how fruit and berries could be grown successfully in the foothills.

Let's not forget James Dodge, who owned a ranch along Humboldt Road a couple of miles above Forest Ranch. Mr. Dodge was making quite a living in what the local newspaper referred to as "a peculiar industry." James would go out into the hills during the spring and gather roots and bulbs from a variety of beautiful wildflowers. After transplanting and growing them on his ranch, he would then sell the bulbs to wholesale florists in this country and abroad. In 1892, he sold more than forty-eight thousand bulbs. In 1893, it was reported that he was growing about half a million bulbs on his ranch. The paper reported that James Dodge was likely the only man in the state who devoted so much energy to this unique business.[287]

The news was still tracking Billy Boness, and the well-known slayer of wild beasts was still having problems with humans. This time, it was in the usually peaceful town of Forest Ranch. Billy had won the affection of a girl, much to the disappointment of Walter Cooper and Harry Dorrett, who circulated an unflattering story about Billy, hoping to dissuade the young lady. A fight ensued, which was quickly suppressed by two other men before any real damage was done.[288]

News about Berdan's place didn't appear in the papers much during this half of the decade, except for occasional reports on the weather or short notes on what the locals were up to.[289] The West Branch and

James Dodge in his later years at Children's Park, Chico. *Courtesy of Shirlon Dodge collection.*

Lomo didn't get much attention either, although the hotel and drinking establishments got a boost when Sierra Lumber decided to construct a new lumber mill nearby.

The Sutton House was still in the news occasionally. Judge Fred Dorrett once came from Forest Ranch to perform a wedding that took place in the woods about half a mile from the Sutton House. The bride was Mary Ellen Silvy and the groom was Joseph Cooper, a mail carrier who will be referred to again soon. It seems Dorrett couldn't perform the ceremony at the planned location because it was in Tehama County and he only had jurisdiction in Butte County. The wedding party moved a short distance into Butte County, and everything was legal. Then everyone went back to the hotel in Tehama County for a grand ball and food.[290]

The McGann hotel continued to be a popular summer resort and place for travelers to rest. James McGann, the proprietor, was reported to be an accommodating and generous person, while his wife was kind and his daughter, Lizzie, was most engaging.[291] Unfortunately, the hotel burned down in November 1893. The hotel, storeroom and saloon were all lost, but the barns were saved.[292] Although it was insured, it's not clear whether a new hotel was ever built. James McGann died three years later.

1890s: Clashing Over Road Maintenance

The Sutton House, circa 1898. *Courtesy of CSU, Chico, Meriam Library, Special Collections.*

Jonesville was still not getting very much attention in the news. The old resort area may have just been past its heyday, as the Butte Meadows area was now getting most of the action. In the summer of 1893, J. Geo. Gibson was traveling through Jonesville and made the observation that Jonesville was more or less deserted, save a few campers, commenting that "'Jones' is not here, neither is his 'vill.'"[293]

In the early 1890s, brothers Louis and Charlie Ruffa settled in the forested meadows on and around Bruce's old place a few miles east of the Big Summit.[294] Louis first established residence sometime in the fall of 1892 and constructed a house and some other buildings. He grazed cattle and grew wild hay.[295] The brothers were finally awarded separate 140-acre land patents in 1918.[296]

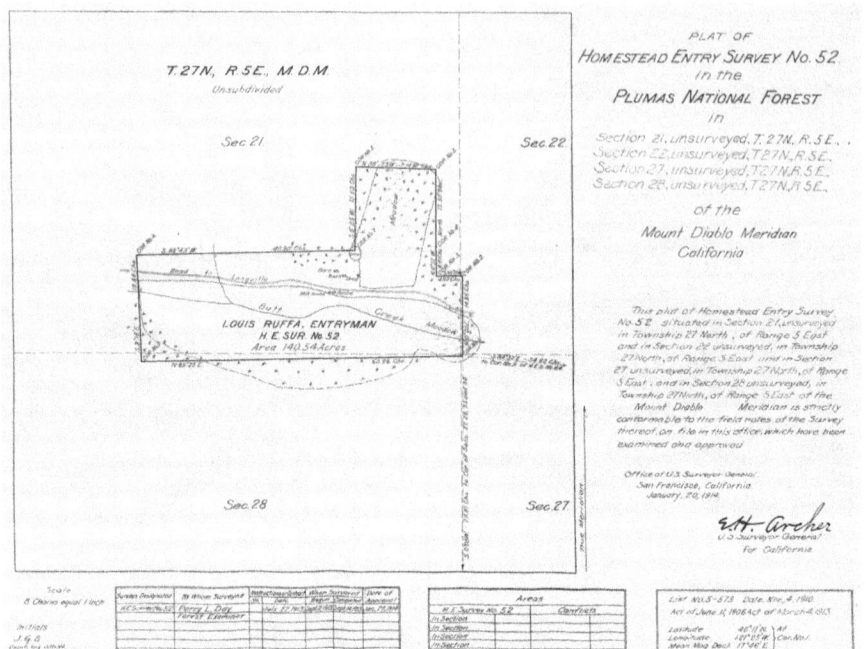

Above: Plat of Homestead Entry Survey no. 52, showing buildings and land boundaries of Louis Ruffa's application for land patent. *Courtesy of BLM GLO Records.*

Left: Charlie Ruffa. His land patent was located about a mile east of brother Louis's. *Courtesy of Chester–Lake Almanor Museum.*

1890s: Clashing Over Road Maintenance

January 1890 was a wet month. Storms created so much flooding in the valley that there was a shortage of stove wood in Chico because the ground was too saturated to haul the fuel in from the nearby fields where it was cut.[297]

In the mountains, they were getting snow from these same storms, and lots of it. Joe Cooper, who carried the mail from the Sutton House to Prattville, barely escaped with his life after being stranded in the snow for an extended length of time and was reported missing when he was not heard from in over a week. His worried friends feared he had perished in the elements.[298] However, Bruce Mason, who carried the mail from Powellton to Prattville on the Humbug Road, reported that he met Cooper in Prattville after the ordeal and related that Cooper was still having trouble recovering. A few weeks earlier, Mason said he got lost and stranded in the snow himself and had to resort to walking around a large pine tree all night, beating himself with switches to keep from freezing to death.[299]

In January 1890, it was reported that Wm. H. Sherwood made three sets of iron snowshoes for Johnny Veal's horses. The new, improved shoes were twelve inches square and were held together with an iron clasp. They had holes in them to allow for horseshoe corks. A strong leather bottom prevented the shoes from slipping. Veal told the paper these should help his teams make good time.[300]

When we think about the postal service, it may remind us of the motto "Neither snow, nor rain, nor heat, nor gloom of night, stays these couriers from the swift completion of their appointed rounds." Was this commitment ever in jeopardy on the Humboldt Road during these times? It seems so. In early 1892, a series of articles printed in the *Chico Enterprise* noted how the Chico to Big Meadows mail wasn't going through and was stranded at either Butte Meadows or Powellton. Apparently, there was a shortage of carriers for a time. One report suggested that the men who were hired to carry the mail were not getting paid, and the contractor was to blame.[301]

Recall that the final settlement in the lawsuit by the government against the Sierra Lumber Company, which was tried in the previous decade, was essentially no more than a slap on the wrist. Nonetheless, Sierra Lumber admitted guilt with no fraudulent intent. In 1891, Sierra Lumber had to deal with timber theft itself and put out a notice in a local paper offering a $500 reward for the arrest and conviction of any person cutting wood on its land without permission in Lassen, Plumas, Tehama, Butte and Shasta Counties.[302] You know what they say, "What goes around comes around."

Barney Cussick was still the mountain manager for Sierra Lumber Company's Chico division, at least for the first half of the decade. In 1890, a news article indicated that there was a plan in the works to close down the Smoky Creek Mill at the end of the logging season and move the machinery elsewhere.[303] However, the New Arcade Mill continued on and, in 1894, was reported to be cutting an average of eighty-nine thousand feet per day during one workweek. Dock Bispham was the head sawyer.[304]

Unfortunately, tragedy struck the Cussick family once more and reminded everyone of how fragile life could be back then, especially in regard to young children. In 1892, Barney's eleven-year-old son, Bernie, died from malignant diphtheria, which originally appeared to be nothing more than a bad cold. The young lad was laid to rest in the mountains next to his sister Maggie.[305]

Of course, accidents and injuries associated with the lumber business were still common during the first half of the decade. Both workers, who were supposed to be on the flume, and recreationalists, who were not, had noteworthy falls. Slipping off the walkway or a board giving way was often the cause.[306] Wayward logs also prompted reportable accidents,[307] as did tramways.[308] One man lost a thumb in a cant hook incident.[309]

Sometimes the injured were sent down the flume to Chico for quick medical attention. Sometimes they were brought down the road in a rig.

The flume inspired people to do risky things, like sit on the edge about sixty to eighty feet above the ground. *Courtesy of CSU, Chico, Meriam Library, Special Collections.*

1890s: Clashing Over Road Maintenance

Just being near the flume inspired some people to take chances. *Courtesy of CSU, Chico, Meriam Library, Special Collections.*

Man standing on precipice with flume below him, across from where the Bidwell Park Golf Course clubhouse is located today. *Courtesy of CSU, Chico, Meriam Library, Special Collections.*

Other times, a doctor might be summoned, although it was once estimated that it would take Dr. Jackson at least seven hours to make the thirty-seven-mile trip mostly uphill from the town of Chico to the New Arcade Mill in Chico Meadows to attend to a severely injured saw worker who had a broken and badly cut leg.[310]

In 1895, big changes were in the works for the Sierra Lumber Company. The New Arcade Mill ran out of nearby trees to harvest, so a new mill in Big Chico Creek Canyon, near the confluence of Campbell Creek, was constructed to replace it. During the winter, the machinery and much of the framework was moved from the old site to the new one.[311] Thirteen miles of flume was abandoned, and a short spur was added from a point below the new mill.[312] The thirty-seven-mile flume was now twenty-five miles long.

The new lumber mill was located alongside the creek about one and a half miles from the West Branch stage stop. The sawmill was aptly named the West Branch Mill, due to its proximity to the Humboldt Road way station, although it was sometimes referred to as Cussick's Mill or, later, the Providence Mill. (It seems that all the mills that Barney Cussick supervised were at one time or another referred to in the press as Cussick's Mill.)

WASHINGTON'S BIRTHDAY IN FOREST RANCH

The snowy winter of 1890 inspired the residents of Forest Ranch to celebrate Washington's Birthday in a memorable way. The festive occasion was described by a correspondent to the *Chico Daily Enterprise* and printed in the February 24, 1890 edition of the paper:

> *Just a few lines to let you know how we are progessing* [sic] *after another snow storm. The beautiful is at this moment, about 18 inches deep, and appearances would seem to indicate that we have had our quota for this time, and we are glad of it.*
>
> *Some of us had hoped to be in Chico to witness that most interesting ceremony to-day, the raising of the glorious "stars and stripes" over your schoolhouses, but the snow storm must be blamed for our absence.*
>
> *Remembering that this was Washington's Birthday W. Shuffleton and W. Holderbaum doubled teams and hooked to an enormous sleigh, (our great Eastern,) then gathering up the sweet young Misses and sturdy young Masters took all for a ride. The patriotic little dears had "old glory"*

flying at the top of a 10-foot flag staff. After the party had visited Mr. Dodge at the Eighteen Mile House, your correspondent had the pleasure of entertaining them; and a short time was very pleasantly spent in singing a number of patriotic and other songs, Miss Bessie Collins and Miss H. Cate leading, to the accompaniment of the guitar.

More Accidents on the Road

Naturally, accidents on the road continued. The area around the Big Summit was the scene of two reported mishaps during the first half of the decade. In one of them, W.P. Sherman was chastising his horse when the equine took umbrage and kicked him hard, dislocating his shoulder joint and breaking his arm.[313] In the other accident, a horse did not fare so well, as told in the May 26, 1890 *Chico Daily Enterprise*:

A horse and buckboard went over Robbers Roost near the Summit, Saturday, and now lie several hundred feet below the grade, a mangled mass of horseflesh and broken buggy.

A man by the name of Jackson was on his way from Susanville to Chico, with a buckboard and three horses. When near the foot of the summit on the other side, he engaged a guide to pilot him over the snow. All traces of the road were lost after he reached the top, and he was picking his way along the edge of the cliff—when the snow gave way and precipitated one of the horses and buckboard to the bottom several hundred feet below. Jackson made his way to Chico with the remaining horses. He placed his loss at $250.

John Decker was "handling the ribbons" on a stage carrying seven passengers when he was forced to employ an unusual method to stop the vehicle. The August 2, 1890 *Chico Weekly Chronicle-Record* explained:

Arriving at the new grade between the Hog Spring and the Ten-Mile House, by some means the brake got out of order and the driver could not manage the craft with so much head wind and no rudder. So he steered as best he could, looking for an opportunity to bank the stage. After several narrow escapes along the sides of the rock-bound roadway, with a solid lava wall on one side and a perpendicular precipice on the other, the stop was attempted and successfully made. We say successfully, although it

Decker's runaway stage accident occurred at or near here, the County Seat Grade, circa 1880. *Courtesy of CSU, Chico, Meriam Library, Special Collections.*

Close-up view of the County Seat Grade, circa 1890. *Courtesy of CSU, Chico, Meriam Library, Special Collections.*

1890s: Clashing Over Road Maintenance

resulted in the upsetting of the stage. Of the seven passengers none were hurt more than slight bruises. The lamp on the side of the coach was smashed and a jug of whiskey broken. Things were soon put to rights and the craft went on its voyage over the billowy Humboldt road, leaving no trace of the disaster except the smell of whiskey on the rocks.[314]

ANOTHER SCARY BEAR STORY

It seems as if this book is not short of stories about scary bear encounters, so why stop now? By the early 1890s, young Albert Harris was building quite a reputation for himself, possibly even supplanting Billy Boness as the premier wild game hunter in the area. The July 1, 1890 *Chico Daily Enterprise* explained:

Albert Harris, an expert young hunter at Forest Ranch, though but 23 years of age, lays claim, and justly, to the fact that more wild game has fallen by his rifle, than by that of any other hunter in the mountains. The young man had an experience a few weeks ago with three large bears that he will not soon forget. He had noticed by tracks in the fruit orchard, that two or three of these animals had been around; so loading his gun, and taking

These bear hides were proudly hanging on the side of a barn at Berdan's, circa 1890.
Courtesy of CSU, Chico, Meriam Library, Special Collections.

133

the dogs with him, followed the trail for several miles, and soon succeeded in treeing one of the varmints. A shot quickly dispatched the animal, and laying his gun down at the foot of a tree, young Harris proceeded to cut Bruin up. While totally unsuspicious of danger, there was a crackling of the brush,—an ominous growl,—and two more full grown bears rushed upon the hunter. He had just time to swing himself into a small pine tree, as the bears reached for him. The dogs ran away on first approach of the animals, and Albert bid fair to remain all night in the tree. The animals squatted down near their dead companion, seemingly willing for the young man to come down. He adopted a novel expedient of reaching his rifle, and adding two more hides to his large collection. He tied his knife to a long string, and after repeated throws, succeeded in wrapping it around the gun, and drawing it to him. A few well directed shots put an end to the bears, and Albert was soon on his way home with his trophy.

Lizzie McGann

Pres Longley and his wife, Maggie. They were married in 1882. She died of consumption in 1887.
Courtesy of CSU, Chico, Meriam Library, Special Collections.

Lizzie McGann was the daughter of one-time Butte County surveyor and hotel proprietor James McGann. Pres Longley was a local poet whose verse was published in Butte County, Sacramento and San Francisco papers. The topics of Longley's writings varied, but many of his poems provide today's reader with a glimpse into the history of California in the 1850s through the early 1900s from the perspective of an educated man who worked a variety of jobs to get by. One of these was as a census taker. When Longley stopped by the McGann hotel in Butte Meadows during his census travels, he was captivated by the proprietor's daughter and was compelled to write a poem about this most charming young lady. The poem was published in the November 20, 1890 *Chico Daily Enterprise*:

1890s: Clashing Over Road Maintenance

For Lizzie McGann

Where the meadows are green, and bright flowers aglow
Where the soft zephyrs sigh and the breeze murmurs low,
Where the tall pines and cedars in majesty stand,
Like sentinels guarding that picturesque land
Dwells Lizzie McGann.

By the pure mountain stream sweeping swiftly away,
Whose crystals are as pure as the sunbeams of day,
Near the cool forest groves where the songs of the birds
Are trilling sweet music, far sweeter than words
Dwells Lizzie McGann.

Her eyes are as blue as the azure above
And her heart is chock full of the sweetest of love
Her voice is as quiet as echoes that play
In the sprite haunted vales at the dawning of day
Dear Lizzie McGann.

Like her mother before her she'll make a good wife
And charm with her presence some lucky man's life
May Heaven's kind blessings that fall in life's span
Give sweetest contentment to Lizzie McGann.
Pres Longley.

In 1892, Lizzie married John Cussick,[315] Barney's younger brother. John took over the reins as superintendent of the West Branch Mill immediately after Barney retired from the lumber business, which was shortly after the mill was built in Big Chico Creek Canyon.[316]

J.H. Shuffleton Dukes It Out in Print

At some point, maintenance and repair of the portion of the Humboldt Road that was Butte County's responsibility was made a political position. This did not come without controversy. In 1890, J.H. Shuffleton of Forest Ranch and C.W. Platt from Lomo ran against each other for the "political office" of road overseer for Butte County District 17,[317] which would be decided by voters in the November election. Shuffleton won the position over both his challengers (W.D. Abbott also entered the race),[318] and Platt was awarded a contract for the upper half of the forty-two-mile stretch that, at one time, Shuffleton had total control over.

Hard feelings between the two road workers ensued. In early 1891, Shuffleton spoke at a road overseer meeting and said that Platt's portion was only in fair condition and claimed that the road overseer could do a better job at that end of the road, and for less money.[319] Platt later defended himself in the newspaper and said his end of the road was in better condition than anytime Shuffleton was maintaining it and equally as good as Shuffleton's end. Platt produced cost figures taken from court records to support his claim that Shuffleton was spending way too much of the county's money on road work.[320] It didn't take long for Shuffleton to shoot back with a letter to the press defending his costs, detailing Platt's alleged failings at the upper end and referring to the contractor "as a joke on our district."[321]

Who figured road maintenance could lead to so much mudslinging? It's no wonder the road overseer became a political position.

In 1892, a new road law eliminated the political office of road overseer in all counties of California, beginning in January 1893.[322] Bids were still accepted, and contracts were awarded to the lowest responsible bidder by the board of supervisors in each county, which also determined the size of the road districts. Each district had a separate contract.[323]

During the summer of 1893, J. Geo. Gibson made a trip over the Humboldt Road and wrote about his experience for the news. Along with some pleasant things about his time in the mountains, he included some rather harsh comments about the condition of the thoroughfare. The August 19, 1893 *Chico Weekly Chronicle-Record* printed what the correspondent referred to as a "piece of my mind":

> What shall I say about the road to Prattville? Here you have nature unadorned! We have heard of the "rocky road to Dublin" and we have been told that "the way of the transgressor is hard," but the road to Dublin

1890s: Clashing Over Road Maintenance

> *with its rocks, and to the other place with its hardness are nothing compared with the road to Prattville. Wherever nature takes a notion to be rough and rocky she is allowed to keep that notion. I thought the "giant's causeway" was in Ireland but it is not. There are boulders in the middle of the road on which your horse dances like a clown until you wonder whether he is going tail first or head first. After you get him properly balanced, you go on a little way breathing a prayer of thanksgiving that your ribs are not broken, when the same performance has to be repeated. If I thought there was the least chance of traveling this road again in the future I would live on bread and water for a week and give the board money thus saved to the county to buy powder to blow up at least a few of the rocks in the middle of the road.*

Shortly afterward, Shuffleton, still the main man for Butte County's Humboldt Road maintenance, took offense to the accusations made by Gibson and didn't hesitate to speak his mind in a local paper. Shuffleton pointed out that Gibson was not clear about what part of the road he was talking about but said the reader might infer that the horseman was referring to the entire road between Chico and Prattville. Shuffleton assured the paper that there was nothing wrong with the Butte County section of the road and suggested that Gibson was not one to make a sound judgment. Shuffleton's take was printed in the August 25, 1893 *Chico Enterprise*:

> *The reverand [sic] gentleman must be very unaccustomed to mountain travel. This is very apparent from his description of his horse, for very surely no man who had ever been over a mountain road would go with a horse that danced like a clown on the boulders until you wondered if you were going head or tail first. It would be interesting to know which of your interesting liverymen perpetrated that joke on the gentleman. He says, "the way of the transgressor is hard." Does this have any reference to the hard way that he seems to have found?*

ATTEMPTED RAPE ON THE BIG SUMMIT

We've read plenty about robberies and accidents on the Humboldt Road, but here's a new twist—an attempted rape by a "foot-pad" (a road criminal who operates on foot rather than horse) at the Big Summit. A chilling description of the attack was told in the September 2, 1893 *Chico Weekly Chronicle-Record*:

> Mrs. James Keefer and her daughter of Chumway, Lassen county, had a fright while coming over the Big Summit Wednesday evening which they will not soon forget. A German foot-pad gave them a close chase for more than two miles in his effort to commit a rape on the daughter.
>
> He first attacked them just beyond the last elevation on the summit and tried to drag the girl, who is about 18 years of age, out of the buggy, and at the same time indecently exposing his person to view.
>
> But the women escaped him and drove up the summit, only to be attacked by the rape fiend again at the first turn in the grade on this side of the summit. This time the brute came near dragging the girl from the buggy, having her almost half way out over the back of the seat when Mrs. Keefer struck him across the face with the buggy whip and then put the whip to her horse, at the same time putting her arm around about her daughter to hold her in the buggy.
>
> The fellow had his arm about the girl's waist and also held her by the arm and it is certainly a wonder that she was not dragged out of the buggy and outraged.
>
> But the fiend was shaken from his hold upon the girl and thrown down in the road and the two women proceeded on their way. But at the next turn in the grade, which is known as the double, the fellow again tackled them. This time, however, he did not get a firm hold upon the girl and Mrs. Keefer put the whip to her horse and ran him all the way to Jonesville, the home of J.F. Dunn and R.K. Dunn and family, where the women told of their experience.
>
> J.F. Dunn, R.K. Dunn and Chas. Baker were at the house and they watched the road for the rape fiend. He came along late in the evening and was captured. After being guarded all night he was brought to Chico by R.K. Dunn last evening on the stage and is now locked up in the City Prison.
>
> Mrs. Keefer swore to a complaint charging him with attempted rape. He will probably have his preliminary hearing before Judge Warren this morning. He is a German and appeared to be about 40 years old. He was enabled to attack the women so often on the summit grade by cutting across between the turns in the road while they had to drive round.
>
> The fellow will probably try to work the crazy dodge.

Although initially refusing to talk or give his name to the authorities, the prisoner finally opened up to reporters, giving his name as Jo. Walters. At first, the man denied any wrongdoing, although he admitted to seeing the

1890s: Clashing Over Road Maintenance

Jonesville Hotel, circa 1909. It is believed that it was originally a one-story structure, and the second story may have been added in the 1880s. *Courtesy of CSU, Chico, Meriam Library, Special Collections.*

women on the road and noticing that they screamed as they passed him, although he did not know why.[324]

Walters was known in Chico, as he had been working on a ranch there for three months. He was regarded as quiet and peaceable.[325]

When first arraigned, the prisoner pleaded not guilty, and his trial was set for later in the month.[326] Before it got that far, though, Jo. Walters pleaded guilty to a charge of attempted rape on the person of Miss Della Keefer. Consequently, he received a sentence of five years in the state prison. His reason for committing the unspeakable crime was free room and board. He was tired of knocking around and trying to scratch out a living. He wanted the taxpayers to take care of him for a while.[327]

MATTIE WARFIELD HAS CLOSE CALL, EVENTUALLY RUNS OUT OF LUCK

Mattie Warfield lived with her parents and siblings about four miles from Chico on a ranch near Butte Creek. One day, Mattie and a younger brother and sister had a close call on their way home from Chico that may have served as a bad omen for what lay in store for them.

The near miss was reported by the March 2, 1895 *Chico Weekly Chronicle-Record*:

> *Mattie Warfield, the seventeen-year-old daughter of George Warfield, who resides at the Spanish Ranch, came to town yesterday with her little brother and sister, and before getting out of town, had a run-away in which the elder Miss Warfield had a most narrow escape from being killed. The young folks had started for home, and when they reached Little Chico creek, on Humboldt avenue, decided to let their horse have a drink out of the creek. After he had finished drinking, the animal became frightened, turned around suddenly, tipping the buggy over on its side and throwing the occupants out on the ground. Mattie's foot caught on the buggy and she was dragged several yards, but fortunately, just before the horse plunged into the creek where the water was about four feet deep, the girl's foot became free and she was left on the bank. The horse ran down the center of the creek for quite a distance and got into a road. The buggy was a complete wreck.*
>
> *The horrifying scene presented in the early part of the runaway was witnessed by a dozen or more people who thought that Mattie Warfield would surely be killed. As it was, none of the children were more than bruised and scared.*

Mattie and her two siblings escaped a brush with catastrophe on that occasion, but their luck would soon run out. Almost two months later, Mattie and two younger siblings (likely the same as earlier) were riding on a buggy on their way to school in Chico when they attempted to cross Butte Creek a few hundred yards from their house. The water was running high and the buggy capsized, dumping the three children into the swift stream. None of them survived. Since there were no witnesses this time, it was speculated that they may have hit the ford, which had been safely crossed many times before, at a bad angle. The current likely swept them to a deep hole nearby that tipped them over. Despite these two mishaps, Mattie was known to be fairly adept at handling horses.[328]

1890s: Clashing Over Road Maintenance

Don't Mess with Earnest Bilby Collins

Of course, there were still robberies reported on the road. A veterinary surgeon was returning from Quincy to Chico in his wagon one day when, near Lomo, a bandit relieved the doctor of about fifty or sixty dollars. Fortunately, the robber left the victim with his watch and chain.[329]

Not all robberies were successful, though, especially for two foot-pads who tried to hold up Earnest Bilby Collins, a savvy student of the law, in Chico. The March 30, 1895 *Chico Weekly Chronicle-Record* related the rather humorous account:

> *If there are any daring foot-pads in Chico, who are looking for a snap, they musn't* [sic] *fool with E. Bilby Collins, for he had an experience Monday with a pair of crooks, and showed himself thoroughly equal to the emergency. Bilby resides on Humboldt avenue, but usually spends three hours in Attorney Henshaw's office each evening in studying law. He then wends his way homeward.*
>
> *Monday night it was about 10 o'clock when he came near Turner's barn on Humboldt avenue, and his thoughts upon a knotty legal proposition were interrupted by the gruff semi-command: "Give me a match, young fellow."*
>
> *Bilby was startled when he saw the forms of two men, one with a club in his hand, and neither not more than five feet away from him. He offered the man without a club a match, but it was refused, and he then tendered it to the "pal" who accepted. Both of the men acted suspiciously and Bilby started homeward as quickly as possible. He had gotten away only a few paces when one of the fellows shouted: "Hold up your hands, young fellow!"*
>
> *Bilby pulled out a metal match-box and aimed it at one of the "pads," and commanded him to make tracks. His command was obeyed, but the other fellow remained stationary. Collins drew the match-box on the remaining hobo, gave him some good advice which was to the effect that he was in bad business, and would some day get caught or hurt. He also advised him that in crimes of that sort the courts are not disposed to be lenient and it is also difficult for the defendant to get able counsel unless he has some spare change. As to the extreme penalty for robbery he gave the hobo no definite information, as the later was in a hurry to move on for fear the match-box might go off.*

Collins admitted that he was nervous and, after it was all over, made haste for home. It was a scary encounter for the young man, but it's possible that bluffing experience may have proved helpful in his future profession.

STORIES OF THE HUMBOLDT WAGON ROAD

RUNAWAY ON THE TRAMWAY

The New Arcade Mill had a near miss one day. The October 3, 1891 *Chico Weekly Chronicle-Record* described the scene:

> *Monday evening about 5 o'clock Scott Knowles, who had charge of the logging cars on the tramway leading to the mill in Chico Meadows met with an accident by which he was slightly bruised and the logging train wrecked. When in about 500 yards of the lower end of the tramway Knowles lost control of the brakes and the cars gained a great velocity. Knowles either jumped or fell off of the car and the train passed on until it reached the turn around the edge of the mountain about 200 yards above the mill. There one of the heavy logs became loosened and plunged butt foremost in front of the lead car, breaking the tramway up for a considerable distance and hurling the fast-flying train to the ground below, a distance of about twenty feet, completely wrecking them. Had the train not been stopped before reaching the mill that structure would have been totally wrecked, as the tramway leads almost directly to the center of the mill and immediately over the engines.*

New Arcade Mill, showing a tramway with a load of logs ready to be dumped onto a rollway. *Courtesy of CSU, Chico, Meriam Library, Special Collections.*

1890s: Clashing Over Road Maintenance

Mountain Men on City Bikes

After the work of transferring the machinery and framework from the mill in Chico Meadows to the new site in Big Chico Creek Canyon was complete, a number of lumberjacks came down from the mountains to spend some time in Chico before returning to work in the higher elevations when the weather became more cooperative.

While in Chico, some of the boys decided to entertain themselves by trying their hands at learning how to ride a bike. Although the following story was meant to be humorous, the reader may also sense the underlying racism that still existed against the Chinese during that time period. The February 9, 1895 *Chico Weekly Chronicle-Record* tells the story:

> *The Sierra Mill boys are having a vacation and they are improving their time in Chico by learning to ride bicycles. They were on dress parade yesterday, and everyone who had been given a cue that they would display their knowledge of the treacherous wheels, was anxious to see how loggers, sawyers and bull drivers would appear astride a modern vehicle.*
>
> *Thomas Slattery, better known at the mill as "Brigham" made his debut at the Park Hotel but had gotten away only a few feet when he went headlong.*
>
> *Bobbie Nicholson had gotten a full head of steam on and in trying to dodge Ah Fong, struck the Mongolian a dead center, picking the Chinaman from under his hat, in "presto change" manner. Phil McGreigan, Bert Brown, James Smith, Grant Fields and John Beall made fun for bystanders by tumbling all along Main street.*

Epilogue

After thirty years of hard use, the road had deteriorated considerably, and near the end of the century, parts of it finally received a major overhaul that was so desperately needed. In 1897, a road improvement project commenced that lasted more than a year. More than one hundred individuals and businesses contributed in one way or another, and new grades were made around six of the steepest hills. It was reported that the county paid $2,010.00 and the people contributed $2,068.05.[330]

Another big event that occurred during the second half of the 1890s was when the hotel at Berdan's burned to the ground, and Myron Berdan suffered burns by saving items from the post office. A local paper reported a touching story about how the locals wasted no time in coming to the assistance of Mr. and Mrs. Berdan, offering provisions, clothes, cooking utensils, dishes and various conveniences to help them cope during this time of difficulty.[331]

The new West Branch Mill generated quite a bit of traffic on the road, until it cut its last log in 1906. Diamond Match Company bought the Sierra Lumber Company the following year, and the V-flume in Big Chico Creek Canyon was completely abandoned. Diamond's mill, located in Stirling City east of Butte Creek, built a network of rails to reach the waiting timber beyond. From the late 1920s to mid-1930s, one of these railroad branches used huge hoists to lower cars down the steep canyon wall of the east side of Butte Creek and then up the steep wall of the west side of the canyon, and vice versa, to harvest trees on the west side of the waterway, which included the area on the Humboldt Road surrounding the old West Branch way station. At the time of this writing,

Epilogue

Sierra Pacific Industries owns most of the land surrounding the Sierra Lumber mills described in this book.

In 1933, the part of the Humboldt Road from the Junction in Chico to the site of Lomo was adopted into the state highway system as State Route 47. Despite the addition of pavement, for many years, it was a treacherous road for automobiles to navigate with its narrow roadbed, sharp curves and lack of safety features (no guardrails or painted stripes and only a few reflectors), just waiting for an accident to happen. Meeting oncoming big trucks around blind curves could be particularly hazardous. By 1970, the modern highway, State Route 32, completely replaced State Route 47, and the road was much improved. Today, it boasts smooth riding most of the way along this stretch, although one may still have to show patience when passing a slow driver.

The old Humboldt Wagon Road still reveals remnants of its former days, with some of the worn-down thoroughfare, the ruts within and rock walls to hold up the roadbed visible at points along the way. Humboldt Avenue (in Chico), Humboldt Road and Highway 32 more or less trace the old path until Lomo, where the old road diverges from the modern highway and identifies itself as the Humboldt Road once more. The pavement ends a little way past Jonesville, and then a dirt and gravel road takes you the rest of the way to Highway 89 on the west side of Lake Almanor, formerly Big Meadows. After a short distance, the old road becomes submerged under the lake for a few miles. After reappearing, it works itself northeast past Clear Creek before eventually catching up with modern Highway 36 near the town of Westwood and more or less following that route the rest of the way to Susanville.

Hog Springs still has water flowing part of the year, but there is not much else there, except for a concrete slab that was constructed in the early 1960s to cover the springs and what's left of a water trough across the road that was made by the Diamond Match Company. The site of Ten-Mile House has residences nearby, but there appears to be no obvious signs of the old way station that used to have water hauled up from the canyon below. Fourteen-Mile House is now a housing development with a historical marker placed in front of it. The small town of Forest Ranch is the first stop out of Chico that has a post office and a store with groceries and other household items for sale. Berdan's is now the site of a CAL Fire station, with some homes nearby. The West Branch is totally abandoned, though it is occasionally used as a modern-day logging camp. Lomo, today located at the northern end of the Hog's Back, has a few occupied dwellings. Butte Meadows is a year-round community that carries on the tradition of attracting visitors from the valley for various recreational activities and escaping the summertime heat

Epilogue

Contemporary photo of rock support for the old road, located just below Fourteen-Mile House. *Photo by author.*

Contemporary photo of Jonesville Hotel, which looks much like it did in the old days, other than it now has a metal roof. *Photo by author.*

Epilogue

Contemporary photo of what's left of a building at Hardin City. *Photo by author.*

of the lower elevations. Chico Meadows is the site of Camp Lassen, a Boy Scout camp. Jonesville has summer cabins and still has the old hotel that is sometimes open to visitors. Beyond Jonesville, there isn't much left alongside the road, except for some abandoned wooden structures, likely built after 1900, at the Ruffa ranch.

You may decide to see for yourself what's left of the road, although much of it has been buried under pavement, submerged by water or simply obliterated over time by erosion. During the summer and fall months, most durable vehicles can easily make it from Chico to Lake Almanor, although the section just below the southwest side of the Big Summit may be a bit challenging for lower clearance vehicles. The road from Jonesville to Lake Almanor, especially the area around the Big Summit, is generally closed to traffic during the winter and early spring, due to the amount of snow.

If the Black Rock Desert is your destination, it would behoove you to take a rugged vehicle, preferably four-wheel-drive, and pack lots of water. From Susanville, the road to Idaho more or less followed the Noble's Emigrant Trail to the Black Rock Desert. Double Hot Springs and Hardin City are located on the west side of the Black Rock Range.

Appendix 1
Truth or Fiction

The following is an amazing story written about a young lady who was part of the Lucas family. Recall that the Lucases owned a ranch some fourteen miles up the Humboldt Road, located a short way below the Fourteen-Mile House. Written under the caption "A Girl's Daring Ride," the correspondent's story was published in the January 28, 1889 *Chico Daily Enterprise*:

> *Near Forest Ranch, in the mountains, above Chico, resides a young lady who for grit and pluck we'll take off our hat to every time. The lady in question, Miss Kate Lucas, resides on a mountain ranch with her mother and brothers, the latter being engaged in furnishing the meat used by the large lumber crews high up in the Sierras. Miss Lucas is a tall, lithe and well built girl, with red, rosy cheeks, jet black hair, bright flashing eyes, and is the acknowledged belle of that vicinity. She is an intrepid horsewoman, and rides fearlessly and alone over the mountain slopes, and through the ravines. She scorns a saddle, and at times rides a fiery mustang, without either bridle or blanket, simply using a lariat, the end tied around her horse's head and neck. She is a capital shot with the rifle, and has worsted many of the crack shots there by her unerring aim. She has been out with her brothers hunting, and very rarely failed to bag a deer, or other wild animals, which so abound in that section. Sometimes the young miss assists in capturing the wild cattle when they are required for the market and then the lariat is twirled with a precision that oft put the vaqueros to shame.*

Appendix 1

> *A few weeks ago, after a daring ride after a particularly wild and fleet-footed steer, which showed fight from the start, the young lady laughed at the vaquero who seemed afraid of the animal, and smilingly challenged him to throw a rope over the animal's head and ride him. The vaquero declined with thanks. Miss Lucas then displayed a piece of courage and daring worthy of the ancient Roman arena. Springing from her horse, she went up to the bound and bellowing beast, quickly and deftly tied a rope around his head and neck, then told the vaquero to let him loose. This he did reluctantly, and the enraged steer was quickly on its feet, but equally as quick the fearless lass was on its back. Then commenced a ride that is rarely witnessed. For half an hour the wild chase and ride was continued over hill and dale, through brush and canyon when the steer gave completely out, and the triumphant girl led her captive to the house. It was a bold feat, and the daring rider has made herself famous in that section of the county.*

Wow! That was an amazing story—a young lady riding bareback on a fast and unruly steer for a half hour through brush and rough terrain until the beast finally gave out. It almost seems made up.

That's because it was. The story above was refuted by a reader whose argument was published in the February 11, 1889 *Chico Daily Enterprise* (again under the caption "A Girl's Daring Ride"):

> ED. ENTERPRISE: *Under the above caption, in your last weekly is described, very minutely, the chase and capture of a particularly wild steer, at the Lucas Ranch on the Humboldt road.*
>
> *Now be it known, that your correspondent (whoever he or she may be) has drawn almost entirely on imagination for the production of that lively sketch.*
>
> *Miss Kate Lucas, the heroine of the story, is, undoubtedly, a good horsewoman, but she never rides fiery mustangs, her brothers having plenty of good American horses for that purpose. That she is a capital shot with a rifle is entirely untrue; that she ever went hunting, or bagged a deer, or any other game is also without the shadow of truth. She never does or ever did, use the lariat, in any way.*
>
> *Although a good horsewoman, Kate Lucas most emphatically denies ever having ridden a steer, either wild or tame, and she does not thank your informant for the very doubtful compliment he pays her.*
>
> F.

Appendix 1

The Lucas family had a cabin in Butte Meadows that was referred to as the "Chicken Shack," circa 1890. *Courtesy of CSU, Chico, Meriam Library, Special Collections.*

So, what gives? If the reader wondered whether some of the newspaper stories about wild exploits from that era were ever made up, or at least embellished, this seems to support the notion that, indeed, some were. This one was particularly suspicious because the correspondent was anonymous. In contrast, the Forest Ranch correspondent who disputed the story was identified and had signed letters to the press before.

What about the editor? Was there any culpability there? Most likely. Newspapers possibly embellished a bit to sell more papers. Sometimes they may have filled empty space with questionable stories just to meet a print deadline. Who knows?

Just about every story has at least a kernel of truth in it, and this one was no exception. We know that Kate lived on Humboldt Road with her mother and several brothers. (The eighteen-year-old Kate also resided with a ten-year-old sister at the time.)[332] It's been established that the oldest brother, John, delivered meat to nearby logging camps. Kate was likely a fit and attractive girl. Living on a ranch, it is reasonable to believe that she knew how to ride a horse well. However, the truth appears to end there, and just like with the news today, you can't believe everything you read.

Appendix 1

So, although most of the stories published in the papers in those days were probably truthful to a large extent, there were obviously some that could not be totally trusted. But they could be entertaining nonetheless. Is it any different today?

Appendix 2
Grand Views from the Humboldt Road

The view from the highest point on the road was described by a traveler in the June 25, 1881 *Weekly Butte Record*:

After passing through and above the timber belt and winding our way among the boulders and scrubby undergrowth that cover the hillsides we came to the SUMMIT OF THE SIERRA. Here amid the craggy cliffs and the huge banks of snow that lie in their shade, battling with the piercing rays of the noonday sun, one beholds Nature's grandest handiwork. Looking

Contemporary photo of a view of Lassen Peak from the Big Summit. *Photo by author.*

Appendix 2

south as far as the eye can discern, a line of snow like the midrib of a huge feather plainly marks the course of the summit of the Sierra, while the dark blue line denotes the presence of pinnated ridges tributary to the central ridge. Toward the north is Mount Lassen with her snow covered top rising in serene majesty, her summit being 11,000 feet above the sea's level, while 1,000 feet below, from the foot of an almost perpendicular precipice, gurgles the fountain head of Butt Creek, a tributary of the Feather river.

A view of the valley fog rolling up to the Fourteen-Mile House is eloquently described in the January 19, 1883 *Chico Enterprise*: "The weather is perfectly clear beyond the Fourteen-Mile House. From that point the valley appears as a great ocean in time of a storm, with its great waves of fog rolling and tumbling beneath."

Scenes like that used to appear on a regular basis during the winter months in California. However, Tule fog is occurring less and less, and it's suggested that climate change may be the reason behind it.

Turbulent-looking valley fog spilling into Big Chico Creek Canyon in 1986. *Photo by author.*

Notes

Much of the information in this book can be found in references cited in the bibliography. The author has also chosen to note more specific sources that he feels may benefit the reader even more. With a few exceptions, these include newspapers and dates. Most of the newspaper articles cited were accessed from the California State University, Chico, historical newspaper collection, either by going online or searching through microfilm. Another source was the California Digital Newspaper Collection, an online repository provided by the University of California, Riverside.

Chapter 1

1. *Daily Alta California*, September 24, 1862.
2. *Sacramento Daily Union*, May 18, 1863, recurring ad.
3. *Marysville Daily Appeal*, June 9, 1863, from the *Index*, a Chico paper.
4. *Weekly Union Record*, April 15, 1865.
5. *Chico Courant*, April 28, 1866.
6. *Northern Enterprise*, June 7, 1872.
7. *Chico Courant*, November 18, 1865.
8. Ibid., May 19, 1866.
9. Ibid., June 30, 1866; July 14, 1866.
10. Ibid., July 21, 1866, recurring ad.
11. Ibid., March 3, 1866; May 12, 1866.

12. Ibid., June 9, 1866.
13. *Marysville Daily Appeal*, April 1, 1866; *Chico Courant*, April 14, 1866; May 19, 1866.
14. *Chico Courant*, March 31, 1866, copied from the *Owyhee Avalanche*; September 8, 1866, condensed version from the *Alta*.
15. Ibid., March 22, 1867.
16. Ibid., October 18, 1867, recurring ads.
17. Ibid., August 30, 1867.
18. Ibid., May 15, 1868.
19. Ibid., September 29, 1866.
20. *Northern Enterprise*, June 12, 1869; July 31, 1869.
21. Ibid., July 17, 1869.
22. *Chico Courant*, February 22, 1867.
23. Ibid., July 21, 1866.
24. Ibid., October 27, 1866.
25. Ibid., January 18, 1867.
26. Ibid., August 30, 1867.
27. Ibid., May 12, 1866, recurring ad.
28. Ibid., June 19, 1868.
29. *Northern Enterprise*, December 18, 1869; June 25, 1870.
30. *North Californian*, November 17, 1855.
31. *Chico Courant*, September 15, 1866.
32. *Humboldt Register*, March 25, 1865.
33. Ibid., April 15, 1865.
34. Ibid., March 11, 1865; *Chico Courant*, March 3, 1866; May 12, 1866.
35. *Humboldt Register*, November 11, 1865.
36. Ibid., November 18, 1865.
37. Ibid., November 25, 1865.
38. Ibid., January 20, 1866.
39. Ibid., December 30, 1865.
40. *Chico Courant*, January 13, 1866; *Humboldt Register*, January 13, 1866; *Chico Courant*, February 10, 1866.
41. *Humboldt Register*, March 31, 1866; *Marysville Daily Appeal*, November 20, 1866.
42. *Chico Courant*, March 17, 1866; August 11, 1866, from Washoe City's *Eastern Slope*.
43. Ibid., April 28, 1866.
44. *Sacramento Daily Union*, May 1, 1866; *Humboldt Register*, September 1, 1866; *Daily Alta California*, September 7, 1866.

45. *Chico Courant*, March 24, 1866.
46. *Marysville Daily Appeal*, November 20, 1866.
47. *Humboldt Register*, March 24, 1866; *Sacramento Daily Union*, May 1, 1866.
48. *Chico Courant*, May 12, 1866; April 12, 1867.
49. Ibid., July 21, 1866.
50. Ibid., June 2, 1866.
51. *Humboldt Register*, March 3, 1866; April 7, 1866.
52. *Chico Courant*, June 2, 1866.
53. Ibid., June 23, 1866; June 30, 1866.
54. *Marysville Daily Appeal*, September 12, 1866.
55. *Daily Alta California*, September 6, 1866; September 7, 1866.
56. *Chico Courant*, October 6, 1866.
57. Ibid., December 7, 1866; *Plumas National*, December 8, 1866.
58. *Humboldt Register*, January 26, 1867.
59. *Chico Courant*, January 4, 1867. The *Courant* spelled the institute's name as "Freyberg."
60. Ibid., April 12, 1867.
61. *Sacramento Daily Union*, May 2, 1867, quoted from Susanville's *Sage Brush*, April 13, 1867.
62. *Chico Courant*, June 7, 1867. The *Marysville Daily Appeal*'s June 9, 1867 edition reprinted this article but began by referring to the man as "Prof. Isenbilk."
63. Ibid., June 14, 1867. The reporter wrote that the bake pan process entailed grinding the rock with a hand mortar, placing some of it in a bake pan with the proper chemicals and heating it above a slow charcoal fire.
64. Ibid., July 12, 1867.
65. Ibid., August 2, 1867.
66. Ibid., September 6, 1867.
67. Ibid., September 20, 1867.
68. Chico Gold and Silver Mining Company incorporation papers, California State Archives.
69. *Chico Courant*, October 11, 1867, an article and ad.
70. Ibid., October 18, 1867.
71. *Sacramento Daily Union*, November 22, 1867, reprinted from the *Virginia Trespass*, November 20, 1867.
72. *Chico Courant*, November 22, 1867.
73. Ibid., November 29, 1867, condensed from the *Sage Brush*.
74. Ibid., November 15, 1867.
75. *Humboldt Register*, December 7, 1867.

76. *Chico Courant*, January 24, 1868; *Humboldt Register*, January 25, 1868.
77. *Chico Courant*, April 10, 1868.
78. Ibid., January 17, 1868; February 21, 1868; March 20, 1868; March 27, 1868.
79. *Humboldt Register*, April 4, 1868.
80. *Chico Courant*, August 2, 1867; *Weekly Butte Record*, August 3, 1867.
81. *Chico Courant*, August 16, 1867; *Weekly Butte Record*, August 17, 1867.
82. *Chico Courant*, November 13, 1869; November 20, 1869.

Chapter 2

83. *Weekly Butte Record*, June 25, 1881; July 16, 1881.
84. *Northern Enterprise*, June 27, 1873.
85. *Chico Enterprise*, August 18, 1876.
86. Ibid., May 24, 1878.
87. Ibid., September 17, 1875.
88. Ibid., October 3, 1879.
89. *Northern Enterprise*, November 7, 1873; February 6, 1874; September 4, 1874, recurring ad.
90. *Chico Enterprise*, May 24, 1878.
91. Ibid., August 18, 1876.
92. *Northern Enterprise*, May 30, 1873.
93. Bureau of Land Management, 1873 T25N R3E map, https://www.glorecords.blm.gov.
94. *Northern Enterprise*, October 17, 1873; April 3, 1874, recurring ad.
95. Ibid., May 1, 1874.
96. *Chico Enterprise*, April 26, 1878.
97. *Northern Enterprise*, August 30, 1872.
98. *Weekly Butte Record*, September 25, 1875.
99. *Chico Enterprise*, August 18, 1876; August 17, 1877.
100. *Northern Enterprise*, July 4, 1873.
101. Ibid., March 26, 1875.
102. *Chico Enterprise*, June 18, 1875.
103. Ibid., April 18, 1879; August 1, 1879; *Weekly Butte Record*, August 2, 1879.
104. *Chico Enterprise*, August 22, 1879; September 5, 1879.
105. Ibid., July 2, 1875; *Weekly Butte Record*, July 3, 1875; *Chico Enterprise*, July 23, 1875; August 13, 1875; December 3, 1875.

106. *Weekly Butte Record*, July 1, 1876, recurring ad.
107. *Chico Enterprise*, September 17, 1875.
108. *Northern Enterprise*, July 9, 1870.
109. Ibid., August 13, 1870.
110. *Weekly Butte Record*, September 25, 1875.
111. *Chico Enterprise*, August 17, 1877.
112. Ibid., January 4, 1878.
113. *Northern Enterprise*, September 19, 1873.
114. *Chico Enterprise*, April 12, 1878.
115. *Northern Enterprise*, April 17, 1874.
116. *Chico Enterprise*, February 25, 1876.
117. Ibid., April 14, 1876.
118. Ibid., May 26, 1876.
119. *Northern Enterprise*, January 14, 1871; March 25, 1871, recurring ad.
120. Ibid., August 30, 1872.
121. Ibid., November 1, 1872.
122. Ibid., May 16, 1873.
123. Ibid., September 4, 1874.
124. Ibid., September 11, 1874.
125. *Chico Enterprise*, June 15, 1877.
126. *Northern Enterprise*, August 14, 1874; *Chico Enterprise*, March 31, 1876.
127. *Chico Enterprise*, June 23, 1876.
128. Ibid., February 16, 1877; April 20, 1877; *Weekly Butte Record*, August 4, 1877.
129. *Chico Enterprise*, April 12, 1878.
130. *Weekly Butte Record*, November 20, 1875.
131. Ibid., April 1, 1876.
132. Ibid., April 21, 1877.
133. *Chico Enterprise*, March 10, 1876; August 31, 1877.
134. Ibid., December 8, 1876; December 15, 1876.
135. Ibid., September 6, 1878; *Weekly Butte Record*, September 28, 1878.
136. *Chico Enterprise*, November 1, 1878.
137. *Weekly Butte Record*, December 7, 1878.
138. *Northern Enterprise*, November 14, 1873.
139. *Weekly Butte Record*, December 27, 1879.
140. *Northern Enterprise*, January 22, 1875.
141. *Chico Enterprise*, May 24, 1878.
142. *Weekly Butte Record*, January 19, 1878.
143. Ibid., March 24, 1877.

144. *Chico Enterprise*, April 11, 1879.
145. Rules and Regulations of the Sierra Flume and Lumber Company, Special Collections, MSS 072, box 2, folder 2, California State University, Chico, 17; *Northern Enterprise*, September 18, 1874, recurring notice.
146. *Northern Enterprise*, August 8, 1873.
147. Ibid., March 13, 1874.
148. *Chico Enterprise*, April 11, 1879.
149. *Weekly Butte Record*, December 11, 1875.
150. *Northern Enterprise*, April 2, 1875.
151. *Chico Enterprise*, October 15, 1875.
152. *Northern Enterprise*, March 20, 1874.
153. *Weekly Butte Record*, April 3, 1875.
154. *Northern Enterprise*, April 9, 1875; *Weekly Butte Record*, April 10, 1875.
155. *Weekly Butte Record*, October 16, 1875.
156. *Northern Enterprise*, August 30, 1872.
157. *Chico Enterprise*, June 13, 1879.
158. Ibid., May 24, 1878.
159. Ibid., May 31, 1878. The *Enterprise* earlier reported that the offending animal was a horse.
160. *Weekly Butte Record*, August 31, 1878.
161. *Northern Enterprise*, November 11, 1871.
162. Ibid., July 26, 1872.
163. *Weekly Butte Record*, August 17, 1878.
164. Ibid., July 14, 1877; *Chico Enterprise*, October 19, 1877.
165. *Chico Enterprise*, August 4, 1876.
166. *Weekly Butte Record*, June 17, 1876.
167. *Chico Enterprise*, August 1, 1879.
168. *Northern Enterprise*, August 1, 1873; August 14, 1874.
169. The November 16, 1877 *Chico Enterprise* reported that the three men were riding "in a box," which the two survivors managed to stop before hitting the jam. In this case, the term "box" appeared to be describing a flume boat.

Chapter 3

170. *Weekly Butte Record*, July 16, 1881.
171. *Chico Semi-Weekly Enterprise*, September 9, 1881.
172. *Chico Enterprise*, April 13, 1883.

173. Ibid., April 6, 1883; April 27, 1883; December 14, 1883.
174. Ibid., August 13, 1886.
175. *Weekly Butte Record*, April 10, 1880.
176. *Chico Enterprise*, August 7, 1885.
177. *Weekly Butte Record*, July 16, 1881.
178. *Chico Semi-Weekly Enterprise*, September 7, 1880.
179. Ibid., December 2, 1881.
180. *Chico Enterprise*, October 6, 1882.
181. *Chico Semi-Weekly Enterprise*, March 28, 1882.
182. *Chico Enterprise*, June 30, 1882.
183. Ibid., September 11, 1885.
184. Ibid., September 9, 1887.
185. *Chico Semi-Weekly Enterprise*, April 21, 1882, from Gridley's *Herald*.
186. Ibid., July 9, 1880, recurring ad.
187. Ibid., September 27, 1881, from Oroville's *Mercury*.
188. *Weekly Butte Record*, June 25, 1881.
189. *Chico Enterprise*, August 12, 1887.
190. *Chico Weekly Chronicle-Record*, August 3, 1889.
191. *Chico Semi-Weekly Enterprise*, April 11, 1882.
192. *Chico Enterprise*, August 21, 1885.
193. *Chico Semi-Weekly Enterprise*, May 28, 1880.
194. Ibid., April 8, 1881.
195. *Weekly Butte Record*, July 15, 1882.
196. *Chico Enterprise*, May 16, 1884.
197. Ibid., October 16, 1885.
198. Ibid., August 1, 1884.
199. *Chico Daily Enterprise*, July 19, 1888.
200. *Chico Semi-Weekly Enterprise*, June 11, 1880, recurring ad.
201. Ibid., May 17, 1881, recurring ad.
202. *Chico Enterprise*, August 10, 1883.
203. *Chico Daily Enterprise*, January 18, 1889.
204. Ibid., June 12, 1889.
205. *Chico Weekly Chronicle-Record*, November 14, 1896; *Chico Enterprise*, November 20, 1896.
206. *Weekly Butte Record*, July 16, 1881.
207. Ibid., June 25, 1881.
208. Ibid., April 21, 1883.
209. *Chico Enterprise*, June 1, 1883.
210. *Weekly Butte Record*, June 9, 1883; *Chico Enterprise*, March 5, 1886.

211. *Chico Enterprise*, April 25, 1884; May 2, 1884; May 16, 1884; May 23, 1884.
212. Ibid., July 16, 1886; *Chico Daily Enterprise*, February 24, 1891.
213. *Weekly Butte Record*, June 18, 1881; August 20, 1881.
214. Ibid., July 9, 1881.
215. *Chico Enterprise*, November 17, 1882.
216. Ibid., July 28, 1882.
217. *Chico Semi-Weekly Enterprise*, December 10, 1880.
218. *Weekly Butte Record*, June 4, 1881.
219. *Chico Enterprise*, June 22, 1883, from Red Bluff's *People's Cause*. The *Cause* referred to the mill as the "New Belmont," but it was clearly referring to the mill in Smoky Creek Canyon.
220. *Weekly Butte Record*, April 5, 1884.
221. *Chico Enterprise*, March 27, 1885; *Chico Weekly Chronicle-Record*, November 30, 1889.
222. *Chico Enterprise*, August 4, 1882; *Weekly Butte Record*, August 5, 1882.
223. *Weekly Butte Record*, July 23, 1881; *Chico Enterprise*, April 23, 1886; *Chico Weekly Chronicle-Record*, February 16, 1889.
224. *Chico Semi-Weekly Enterprise*, July 29, 1881; *Chico Daily Enterprise*, May 19, 1888.
225. *Chico Semi-Weekly Enterprise*, August 24, 1880; *Chico Daily Enterprise*, February 5, 1889; February 9, 1889.
226. *Chico Enterprise*, December 2, 1887.
227. *Weekly Butte Record*, August 6, 1881.
228. *Chico Enterprise*, March 7, 1884.
229. Ibid., July 31, 1885.
230. Ibid., July 28, 1882.
231. *Sacramento Daily Union*, July 20, 1885; *Chico Enterprise*, July 24, 1885.
232. *Chico Semi-Weekly Enterprise*, May 28, 1880.
233. Ibid., June 8, 1880.
234. *Weekly Butte Record*, March 25, 1882.
235. *Chico Enterprise*, February 11, 1887.
236. Ibid., February 25, 1887.
237. Ibid., March 4, 1887.
238. Ibid., May 1, 1885; December 4, 1885.
239. Ibid., January 9, 1885.
240. *Chico Semi-Weekly Enterprise*, April 26, 1881.
241. *Chico Enterprise*, December 31, 1886.
242. Ibid., July 8, 1887.

243. Ibid., October 2, 1885.
244. *Daily Alta California*, May 17, 1885, from the *Chico Enterprise* of unknown date.
245. *Chico Enterprise*, May 26, 1882; *Weekly Butte Record*, July 8, 1882.
246. *Chico Enterprise*, October 27, 1882.
247. *Chico Semi-Weekly Enterprise*, June 15, 1880.
248. *Chico Enterprise*, May 26, 1882.
249. *Weekly Butte Record*, May 27, 1882; June 3, 1882.
250. Ibid., June 3, 1882; *Chico Enterprise*, April 6, 1883; April 13, 1883; May 2, 1884; *Chico Daily Enterprise*, January 10, 1888.
251. *Weekly Butte Record*, May 3, 1884.
252. *Chico Semi-Weekly Enterprise*, July 23, 1880.
253. *Chico Enterprise*, December 28, 1883.
254. *Chico Semi-Weekly Enterprise*, June 25, 1880.
255. *Chico Daily Enterprise*, August 2, 1888.
256. *Chico Weekly Chronicle-Record*, March 24, 1888.
257. *Chico Enterprise*, July 14, 1882.
258. Ibid., October 17, 1884.
259. Located in the far northeast corner of California, the fort was named in honor of Congressman John Bidwell, who persuaded the army to provide extra protection for people and property from Indian raids along the road to Idaho.
260. *Chico Enterprise*, April 13, 1883. The *Enterprise* spelled his name as "Moulter."
261. Ibid., June 22, 1883, from Red Bluff's *People's Cause*; October 12, 1883. The *Cause* was referring to the mill in Smoky Creek Canyon.
262. *Chico Daily Enterprise*, July 31, 1888.
263. *Chico Enterprise*, February 19, 1886; *Weekly Butte Record*, February 20, 1886; February 27, 1886.
264. *Chico Enterprise*, October 28, 1887, from the *Sacramento Bee*; November 11, 1887.
265. *Weekly Butte Record*, April 17, 1886.
266. *Chico Weekly Chronicle-Record*, February 11, 1888.
267. *Chico Daily Enterprise*, December 6, 1888.
268. *Chico Weekly Chronicle-Record*, February 2, 1889. Shasta County was also included in the alleged violations.
269. *Chico Daily Enterprise*, December 8, 1888.
270. *Chico Enterprise*, February 1, 1889; *Chico Daily Enterprise*, February 2, 1889.
271. *Chico Daily Enterprise*, April 7, 1891.

Chapter 4

272. *Chico Daily Enterprise*, August 5, 1891.
273. *Chico Weekly Chronicle-Record*, December 26, 1891.
274. *Chico Enterprise*, July 26, 1895.
275. *Chico Daily Enterprise*, February 21, 1891, recurring ad.
276. *Chico Enterprise*, October 9, 1891.
277. Ibid., March 4, 1892; August 12, 1892; November 10, 1893.
278. *Chico Weekly Chronicle-Record*, May 27, 1893.
279. *Chico Daily Enterprise*, October 9, 1890.
280. *Chico Enterprise*, May 8, 1891.
281. Ibid., June 3, 1892.
282. *Chico Daily Enterprise*, February 24, 1890.
283. *Chico Weekly Chronicle-Record*, December 30, 1893.
284. Ibid., July 18, 1891.
285. Ibid., August 5, 1893.
286. *Chico Enterprise*, September 8, 1893; September 15, 1893.
287. Ibid., June 9, 1893, from the *Oroville Mercury*.
288. *Chico Daily Enterprise*, July 20, 1891.
289. *Chico Enterprise*, January 8, 1892.
290. *Chico Daily Enterprise*, June 30, 1891.
291. Ibid., November 20, 1890.
292. *Chico Enterprise*, November 17, 1893.
293. *Chico Weekly Chronicle-Record*, August 19, 1893.
294. *Chico Daily Enterprise*, September 20, 1890. The newspaper reported that Michael Bruce sold the Summit Ranch to "Larger" (likely misspelled) Ruffa.
295. Department of the Interior Homestead Entry No. 02750, final proof, testimony of claimant, National Archives.
296. Louis and Charles Ruffa land patents, https://www.glorecords.blm.gov.
297. *Chico Daily Enterprise*, January 23, 1890.
298. Ibid., January 29, 1890.
299. Ibid., February 1, 1890.
300. Ibid., January 9, 1890.
301. *Chico Enterprise*, February 19, 1892; March 4, 1892.
302. *Weekly People's Cause*, August 15, 1891, recurring notice.
303. *Chico Weekly Chronicle-Record*, September 6, 1890.
304. *Chico Enterprise*, July 27, 1894.
305. *Chico Weekly Chronicle-Record*, July 16, 1892.

306. *Chico Enterprise*, August 15, 1890; *Chico Weekly Chronicle-Record*, September 13, 1890; *Chico Daily Enterprise*, September 15, 1890; *Chico Weekly Chronicle-Record*, September 20, 1890; *Chico Daily Enterprise*, May 20, 1891.
307. *Chico Daily Enterprise*, October 17, 1890; *Chico Enterprise*, August 10, 1894.
308. *Chico Weekly Chronicle-Record*, October 3, 1891; May 14, 1892.
309. *Chico Daily Enterprise*, February 10, 1891.
310. *Chico Weekly Chronicle-Record*, August 15, 1891.
311. Ibid., January 26, 1895.
312. *Chico Enterprise*, February 1, 1895.
313. *Chico Daily Enterprise*, October 31, 1891, from the *Bulletin*, a Plumas County paper.
314. The July 28, 1890 *Chico Daily Enterprise* also wrote about the incident, reporting that the brake block gave way and the stage was delayed six hours.
315. *Chico Enterprise*, June 17, 1892.
316. Ibid., July 26, 1895.
317. *Chico Daily Enterprise*, September 22, 1890, recurring announcement.
318. Ibid., October 11, 1890, recurring announcement.
319. Ibid., February 7, 1891.
320. Ibid., February 24, 1891.
321. Ibid., March 3, 1891.
322. *Chico Enterprise*, May 20, 1892.
323. Ibid., January 13, 1893; February 24, 1893.
324. Ibid., September 1, 1893. The *Enterprise* indicated the girl was about fourteen years old.
325. Ibid., September 8, 1893.
326. *Chico Weekly Chronicle-Record*, September 9, 1893.
327. Ibid., September 30, 1893, from the *Oroville Mercury*.
328. Ibid., April 27, 1895.
329. *Chico Daily Enterprise*, October 2, 1891.

Epilogue

330. *Chico Daily Record*, January 5, 1899.
331. Ibid., April 7, 1898.

Appendix I

332. Tenth Census of the United States, 1880, National Archives and Records Service.

BIBLIOGRAPHY

Publications

Angel, Myron. *Reproduction of Thompson and West's History of Nevada 1881: With Illustrations and Biographical Sketches of Its Prominent Men and Pioneers.* Berkeley, CA: Howell-North, 1958.

Burrill, Richard L. *Ishi's Untold Story in His First World Parts III–VI: A Biography of the Last of His Band of Yahi Indians in North America.* Red Bluff, CA: Anthro Company, 2012.

Butte Meadows–Jonesville Community Association History Committee. *A Small Corner of the West: Butte Meadows, Chico Meadows, Jonesville, California.* Rev. ed. Chico, CA: Butte Meadows–Jonesville Community Association, 1999.

Chang, Anita Louise. "The Historical Geography of the Humboldt Wagon Road." Master's thesis, California State University, Chico, 1991.

Clarke, K.W., ed. "The Humboldt Road." In *California Folklore Chico Collection*, 28–45. Vol. 14. Chico, CA: Chico State College, 1958.

Coy, Owen C., ed. *Pictorial History of California.* Berkeley: University of California Extension Division, 1925.

Fairfield, Asa Merrill. *Fairfield's Pioneer History of Lassen County California.* San Francisco: H.S. Crocker Company, 1916.

Frei, George E. "At Home on the Range: The Biography of John Henry Lucas." Archival research seminar paper, California State University, Chico, 1992.

Gage, Helen Sommer. "The Humboldt Road." In *Butte Remembers*, 9–11. Chico, CA: North Valley Printing & Publishing, 1973.

Gilbert, Frank T. "History of California from 1513 to 1850." In *History of Butte County, California, in Two Volumes*, 57. San Francisco: Harry L. Wells, 1882.

Gillis, Michael J., and Michael F. Magliari. *John Bidwell and California: The Life and Writings of a Pioneer, 1841–1900*. Spokane, WA: Arthur H. Clark Company, 2004.

Hall, Jacqueline, and Jo Ellen Hall. *Italian-Swiss Settlement in Plumas County: 1860 to 1920*. Chico: Association for Northern California Records and Research, 1975.

Hutchinson, W.H. *California Heritage: A History of Northern California Lumbering*. Rev. ed. Santa Cruz, CA: Forest History Society, 1974.

Johnston, Ken. *Legendary Truths: Peter Lassen & His Gold Rush Trail in Fact & Fable*. Greybull, WY: Pronghorn Press, 2012.

Leek, Nancy. *John Bidwell: The Adventurous Life of a California Pioneer*. Chico: Association for Northern California Historical Research, 2010.

Leicester, Marti, and David Nopel. *The Humboldt Wagon Road*. Charleston, SC: Arcadia Publishing, 2012.

Mansfield, George C. *History of Butte County California with Biographical Sketches of the Leading Men and Women of the County Who Have Been Identified with Its Growth and Development from the Early Days to the Present*. Los Angeles: Historic Record Company, 1918.

Mark, Andy. "1859 Butte Creek White Settler–Indian Conflicts." *Diggin's* 54, no. 1 (Spring 2010): 3–20.

———. *The West Branch Mill of the Sierra Lumber Company: Early Logging in Northeastern California*. Charleston, SC: The History Press, 2012.

McGie, Joseph F. *History of Butte County*. Vol. 1, *1840–1919*. Rev. ed. Oroville, CA: Butte County Board of Education, 1983.

McIntosh, Clarence F. "The Chico and Red Bluff Route: Stage Lines from Southern Idaho to the Sacramento Valley, 1865–1867." *Idaho Yesterdays* 6, no. 3 (Fall 1962): 12–19.

Moulton, Hobart. *We Are Not Forgotten: A Narrative History of Eastern Tehama County*. Red Bluff, CA: Tehama County Genealogical and Historical Society, 1987.

Paher, Stanley W. *Nevada Ghost Towns and Mining Camps*. Berkeley, CA: Howell-North, 1970.

Quadrio, Marilyn Morris. *Big Meadows and Lake Almanor*. Charleston, SC: Arcadia Publishing, 2014.

Raymond, Rossiter W. *Mineral Resources of the States and Territories West of the Rocky Mountains.* Washington, D.C.: Government Printing Office, 1869.

Rudderow, John, and Nancy Leek. *The Miner Poet: Poems of Pres Longley.* Chico, CA: Stansbury Publishing, 2013.

Salley, Harold E. *History of California Post Offices, 1849–1976: Includes Branches and Stations, Navy Numbered Branches, Highway and Railway Post Offices.* La Mesa, CA: Postal History Associates, 1977.

Smith and Elliot. *Butte County, California: Illustrations Descriptive of Its Scenery, Residences, Public Buildings, Manufactories, Fine Blocks, Mines, Mills, & C.* Oakland, CA: Smith and Elliot, 1877.

Speer, Robert. "Saving the Jonesville Hotel." *Chico News & Review*, October 6, 2011. https://www.newsreview.com.

Stephens, Kent. *Matches, Flumes and Rails: The Diamond Match Company in the High Sierra.* Corona del Mar, CA: Trans-Anglo Books, 1977.

Straka, Thomas J. "Timber for the Comstock." *Forest History Today* (Spring/Fall 2007): 4–15. https://usminedisasters.miningquiz.com.

Tuchinsky, Evan. "Bearing No Fruit: Studies Explore Climate Change's Effect on Local Agriculture." *Chico News & Review*, March 22, 2018.

Wheeler, Sessions S. *Nevada's Black Rock Desert.* Caldwell, ID: Caxton Printers, 1978.

Whisman, Ernest S. "A Walk from Chico to Honey Lake Valley." *Diggin's* 11, no. 4 (Winter 1967): 3–12.

White, Gregory F., Ron Womack, Nancy Leek, Josie Reifschneider-Smith, David M. Brown and Michelle Rader. *Ten Miles of Roadside Archeology Along the Old Humboldt Wagon Road: A Cultural Resource Investigation of the Santos Fire Area, Upper Bidwell Park.* Chico: Association for Northern California Historical Research, 2018.

Maps

Keddie, Arthur W. *Official Map of Plumas County.* Based on the work of the State Geological Survey, by V. Wackenreuder in 1866, under the direction of J.D. Whitney, state geologist, 1874.

McGann, James, and Britton and Rey. *Official Map of the County of Butte, California.* San Francisco: Lith. Britton, Rey and Co, 1877. https://www.loc.gov.

Mullen, Captain John. *Stage Road from Chico to Boise City.* Map prepared for General McDowell, 1865.

BIBLIOGRAPHY

Shackelford, H.B., F.J. Nugent and Britton and Rey. *Official Map of the County of Tehama, California*. San Francisco: Lith. Britton and Rey, 1878. https://www.loc.gov.

Historical Newspapers

Chico Courant
Chico Daily Enterprise
Chico Daily Record
Chico Enterprise
Chico Semi-Weekly Enterprise
Chico Weekly Chronicle-Record
Daily Alta California
Humboldt Register
Lassen Advocate
Marysville Daily Appeal
North Californian
Northern Enterprise
Plumas National
Sacramento Daily Union
Weekly Butte Record
Weekly People's Cause
Weekly Union Record (Oroville)

Additional Sources

Bureau of Land Management general land office records. https://www.glorecords.blm.gov.
California State Archives.
California State University, Chico, Special Collections MSS 072.
National Archives.
Tenth Census of the United States, 1880. National Archives and Records Service.

INDEX

A

Abbott, W.D. 136
Allen, Taylor and Holbrook 32, 65
Anthony, John 64
Apperson, Dock 91
Arcade Mill 65, 67, 81, 89
Arcade Springs 61
Atchison Mill 48, 49

B

Baker, Chas. 138
Baker, Colonel 61, 62
Baker Spring 62
Bakerville 88
Balch, Billy 93, 94
Barham, Buck 96, 97
Barnard, J.M. 87
Barnard, Mrs. J.M. 88
Bartol, Sol. 80
Bass, L. 45, 46
Beall, John 143
Bellew, J.W. 34, 35, 36
Belmont Mill 65, 67, 80, 81, 89

Bennet, Henry 94, 95, 96
Bennett, George W. 60
Berdan, Mrs. Myron 145
Berdan, Myron 59, 75, 86, 145
Berdan's 59, 64, 86, 123, 133, 145, 146
Bernard, Mr. 103
Bidwell, John 5, 23, 24, 25, 26, 27, 29, 38, 43, 46, 54, 65, 88, 92, 110, 113, 163
Big Meadows (California) 17, 127, 146
Big Meadows (Nevada) 37
Bispham, Dock 128
Black Rock Tom 35, 36, 37
Boness, William (a.k.a. Billy) 73, 105, 106, 123
Bonham, Wm. 59, 86
Boyer, Wash 107, 108
Brightman, E.K. 87
Brightman, Mrs. E.K. 87
Brown, Bert 143
Brown, James 85
Brown, John 85

INDEX

Bruce, Mike 63, 164
Bruce's place 63, 88, 125
Bruce, William 106
Burk, Shorty 113
Butte Flume and Lumber Company 65
Butte Meadows 17, 60, 61, 64, 70, 88, 90, 91, 92, 101, 106, 107, 108, 125, 127, 146, 151

C

Cady, Sheriff Frank 110, 111, 112
Cain, Milton 74, 75, 76
Campbell's station 59, 60
Campbell, Uncle Jo 59
Camper, Miss Molly 107
Canfield's Carriage Shop 98
Carter, J.E. 63, 87, 88
Cascade Mill 65, 67, 89
Cate, Miss H. 131
Cement Springs 29, 54
Chico Gold and Silver Mining Company 45, 46, 47
Chico Meadows 31, 89, 148
Clark, A.T. 34, 53
Cochran, R.M. 26
Colby, G.W. 63, 106
Cole, L.L. 82
Collins, Earnest Bilby 141
Collins, Miss Bessie 131
Comet Mill 32, 74, 75
Cooley, Alex 87
Cooley, Mrs. Alex 87
Cooper, Joseph 124, 127
Cooper, Walter 123
Coppin, Charles 86
Cox, Mr. (old man) 57
Crabb, Mr. 86
Craig, David 57, 86
Craig, James 103, 104

Crum, Cash 122
Crum, Martin 121
Cussick, Barney 89, 90, 97, 118, 127, 128, 130, 135
Cussick, Bernie 128
Cussick, John 135
Cussick, Maggie 118, 128

D

Dall's Mill 41, 45, 47, 49
Daniels, Sheriff 75, 76
Dashaway Mill 58, 86
Davies, Charles (a.k.a. Don Carlos) 74, 75
Davis, T.F. 88
Decker, John 131, 132
Diamond Match Company 67, 145, 146
Dix Mine 96, 99
Dodge, James 123, 124
Dodge, P.H. 88
Dodge ranch 123, 131
Dorland, George 75
Dorland, James 75, 76
Dorrett, Fred 85, 86, 122, 124
Dorrett, Harry 123
Double Springs 43, 148
Dunn, J.F. 88, 138
Dunn, R.K. 138
Duren, W.H. 44, 45, 46
Dye, Ike 51, 53
Dye, Job 63
Dye's ranch 30, 31, 53, 63

E

Elliot, Miss Nettie 81
Ellsworth, C.F. 32, 64
Embry, Wm. 82
Empire Mill 32, 70, 71
Epperson, Henry 109

172

INDEX

Epperson, Mr. 106
Evans and Company Mill 43, 45, 46

F

Feiss, Henry 110, 111
Ferris, Mrs. 57
Fields, Grant 143
Findley, Elias 58, 80
Findley's place 29, 58, 59
Fong, Ah 143
Forest Mill 32
Forest Ranch 59, 64, 86, 106, 107, 108, 109, 121, 122, 123, 130, 133, 146
Fort Bidwell 110, 111, 163
Fourteen-Mile House 54, 57, 63, 86, 121, 146, 147, 154

G

Garland claim 99
Gibson, J. Geo. 125, 136, 137
Good, Hi 27, 28, 52, 53
Guill, John 26

H

Hail, F.G. 80
Hail, Mrs. F.G. 80
Hardin City 43, 46, 148
Hardin, James 38, 50
Harris, Albert 133, 134
Harvey, Judge 41
Hegan, Constable 77
Hill, Henry C. 110, 111, 112, 113
Hiskey, J.B. 47, 49, 50
Hog Springs 13, 29, 57, 80, 85, 121, 146
Holderbaum, W. 130
Humbug Road 5, 28, 53, 123

I

Idaho Stage Company 27
Isenbeck, Professor Charles 41, 44, 45, 46, 47, 48, 49, 50

J

Jackson, Dr. 130
Jackson, Mr. 131
Johnson, Captain 30
Johnson, Frank 44, 45, 46, 47
Jonesville 30, 54, 55, 62, 64, 70, 71, 88, 125, 138, 139, 146, 147, 148
Jud, S.S. 57
Junction 11, 12, 13

K

Keefer, Miss Della 138, 139
Keefer, Mrs. James 138
King, Dr. William 61, 65
Kingsbury, Fred 86, 106, 107
Knight, Isadore 109
Knowles, Scott 142

L

Lassen, Peter 38, 39
Lee's place 74
Lemm, Carl 87
Lomo 60, 61, 64, 87, 124, 146
Longley, Pres 134, 135
Longmore, A.C. 45, 46
Lucas, Ellen 29, 85
Lucas, John (a.k.a. Jack) 121, 151
Lucas, Miss Kate 149, 150, 151
Lucas, Paul 29, 85
Lucas ranch (Big Chico Creek Canyon) 29, 149, 150
Lucas ranch (Butte Meadows) 61

Index

M

Mack, James 31
Mandeville, J.C. 26, 46
Mapes's ranch 110
Martin, J.C. 41, 43, 46
Mason, A.G. (a.k.a. Bert) 115
Mason, Bruce 127
McCargar, Erastus 82
McClusky, Ike 113
McCormick brothers 65
McCormick, J.N. 30
McDonald's place 29, 32
McFadden, Thomas 44, 46
McGann hotel 88, 124, 134
McGann, James 12, 58, 59, 60, 88, 124, 134
McGann, Lizzie 124, 134, 135
McGann, Mrs. James 88, 124
McGann's ranch 30, 61
McGreigan, Phil 143
McVey, James 57, 79, 80, 85
Means, Mr. 60, 61
Means, Mrs. 60
Messer, Mrs. W.N. 103
Messer, W.N. 87, 103
Mickey, Frank 108, 109
Molder, John 113
Morgan, J.C. 76
Morrill, Jo 32
Morrison, Captain John 86, 89, 123
Morrison, Mrs. John 86, 123
Mullan, John 21, 27, 28
Musselman, D.O. 60, 77, 78
Musselman's 59, 60, 77, 78

N

Nelson, Ed. 103
New Arcade Mill 89, 90, 91, 128, 130, 142, 143
Nicholson, Bobbie 143

O

O'Ferrall, R.H. 29
O'Neil, Captain 115, 116
Oregon Steam Navigation Company 28

P

Perkins, John H. 57
Phillips, Mr. 76
Platt, C.M. 96
Platt, C.W. 89, 136
Platt's (C.M.) place 96
Pond, E.B. 26
Portuguese Point 32, 99, 100
Powellton 123, 127
Prattville 5, 17, 18, 31

R

Rancho Chico 24, 25, 92
Rank, Susan (a.k.a. Widow Franklin) 74, 75, 76
Ratcliff, Miss Nona 109, 110
Raymond, Rossiter W. 48
Reavis, D.M. 80
Roberts, W.C. 61, 88
Rogers, Francis 79
Ruby City 27, 28
Ruffa, Charlie 125, 126
Ruffa, Louis 125, 126

S

Sanders, Mr. 78
Saunders's place 29
Scribner and Wiseman 99
Sewell, Mr. 60
Shackelford, Colonel H.B. 65, 66
Sharp, Harry 102

Index

Sherman, W.P. 131
Sherwood, Wm. H. 127
Shirley, H.T. 87
Shuffleton, J.H. 89, 136, 137
Shuffleton's place 123
Shuffleton, W. 130
Sierra Flume and Lumber Company 65, 67, 160
Sierra Lumber Company 67, 68, 69, 89, 90, 119, 120, 124, 127, 130, 145
Sierra Pacific Industries 146
Silvy, Mary Ellen 124
Sims, Jacob Franklin 88
Slattery, Thomas (a.k.a. Brigham) 143
Smith, James 143
Smoky Creek Mill 89, 90, 116, 117, 128, 162, 163
Spencer, A.M. 81
Spencer, Ike 87, 88
Spires family 86
Sprague, James K. 30
Springer, Jason 65
Springer, W.K. 64, 75, 80
Sproul, Dr. 30
Stansbury, Dr. O. 108, 109
Susanville 5, 18, 19, 30, 31, 40, 41, 64, 110, 112
Sutter, John 23, 24
Sutton House 61, 64, 81, 87, 88, 93, 100, 124, 125
Sutton, John 61
Swift, William 81

T

Tehama County Wagon Road 5, 28
Ten-Mile House 57, 58, 79, 80, 85, 121, 146
Thacker, Detective 111, 112
Thomas, D.O. 61
Tickner, Burnham and Company Mill 92
Torrey's Mill 41
Tubbs, Mr. 77, 78
Twitchell, Mr. 78, 79

U

Unionville 34, 40, 41, 44, 47

V

Veal, Johnny 98, 99, 107, 123, 127
Victor Mill 61, 65

W

Wakefield, Henry 30
Wakefield's station 30, 32
Walters, Jo. 138, 139
Warfield, Miss Mattie 139, 140
Washoe City 41, 42
Wayland, Dr. Joseph 93
Weld, Horace D. 58, 86
Weld, Mrs. Horace D. 58
Wertsbaugher, J.C. 29
West Branch Mill 130, 135, 145
West Branch station 60, 64, 86, 102, 123, 130, 145, 146
Wetherbee, Ira A. 46, 47
Wilson, Johnny 103, 104
Woods, Chas. 107
Woods, Mrs. Chas. 107
Woodsum brothers 32, 65

Y

Yelper Mill 60
Young, Alex (a.k.a. Sandy) 51, 52, 53, 64

About the Author

Andy Mark worked as a brakeman and conductor on the Western Pacific and Union Pacific Railroads for twenty-one years before going back to college. He graduated from California State University, Chico, as a double major in mathematics (option in statistics) and psychology. After working sixteen years as a statistical consultant and data analyst, Andy retired in 2013. He was acknowledged in various books and scientific publications for his contributions.

Before retirement, Andy started directing his attention toward local history. He wrote an article titled "1859 Butte Creek White Settler–Indian Conflicts," which appeared in the Butte County Historical Society's spring 2010 edition of the *Diggin's*. He authored a book titled *The West Branch Mill of the Sierra Lumber Company: Early Logging in Northeastern California*, which was published by The History Press in 2012. He subsequently wrote an article titled "How Western Pacific's Scenic Feather River Route Almost Wasn't," which was published in the winter 2013 edition of the *California Territorial Quarterly*.

Andy has enjoyed hiking ever since he was a youth growing up in Northern California. He's explored a lot of the backcountry in Butte, Plumas and Tehama Counties on foot and/or mountain bike, often coming across numerous pieces of evidence left by humans from earlier times. Andy feels his interest in local history helped him find a way to blend an understanding and appreciation for the past with his love of nature.

Andy and his wife, Jill, are longtime rock hounds and have searched many of the western states for stony treasures. This has led them, on many occasions, to the deserts of northwestern Nevada, which inspired them to learn the history of that area.

www.ingramcontent.com/pod-product-compliance
Lightning Source LLC
Chambersburg PA
CBHW042142160426
43201CB00022B/2380